TRACING YOUR
FAMILY HISTORY
MADE
EASY

Contents

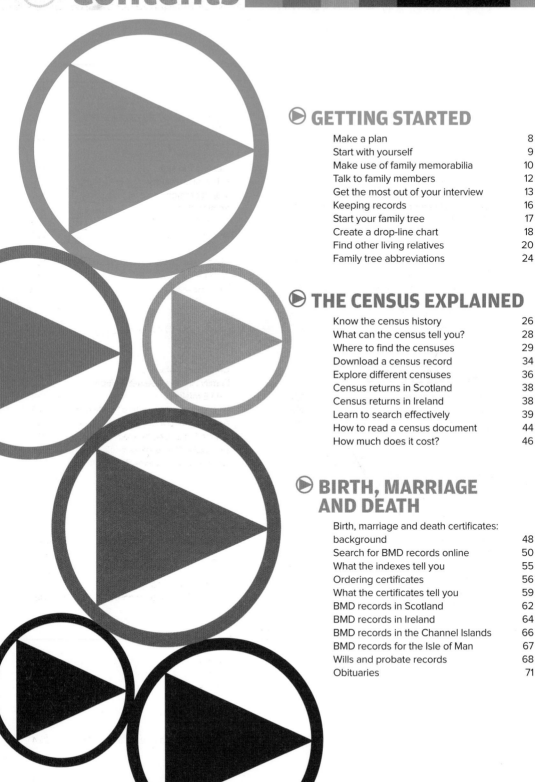

TRACING YOUR FAMILY HISTORY
MADE EASY

Which? Books are commissioned and published by Which? Ltd,
2 Marylebone Road, London NW1 4DF
Email: books@which.co.uk

British Library Cataloguing in Publication Data
A catalogue record for this book is available from the British Library

Picture credits: All photographs courtesy of Shutterstock except for p17: Doreen Pinnell; p38: The National Archives, ref. RG11/1037 f57; p41: The National Archives, ref. HO107-525 Pt3 f10 Census 1841 Chorley; p42: The National Archives; p44: The National Archives, ref. RG13-1122 f118 Census 1901; pp59, 60, 61, 62: Doreen Pinnell

ISBN 978 1 84490 124 1

1 3 5 7 9 10 8 6 4 2

The publishers would like to thank Francesca Bashall, Sarah Kidner, Philippa Neville, Simon Orde and Doreen Pinnell for their help in the preparation of this book.

Consultant editor: Nicola Lisle
Project manager: Emma Callery
Designer: Blânche Williams, Harper Williams Ltd
Proofreader: Kathy Steer
Indexer: Lynda Swindells
Printed and bound by Charterhouse, Hatfield
Distributed by Littlehampton Book Services Ltd, Faraday Close, Durrington, Worthing, West Sussex BN13 3RB

Essential Velvet is an elemental chlorine-free paper produced at Condat in Périgord, France using timber from sustainably managed forests. The mill is ISO14001 and EMAS certified.

For a full list of Which? Books, please call 01903 828557 or access our website at www.which.co.uk, or write to Littlehampton Book Services.

BEFORE CIVIL REGISTRATION

USING ARCHIVES

OCCUPATIONS

DELVING FURTHER

BUILD YOUR TREE ON A PC

GENEALOGY FRIENDS ONLINE

RESOURCES

INTRODUCTION

Family history has become a major national pastime, as more and more people delve into their past and try to find out about their forebears. With the advent of the internet, this research has never been easier, and much of the information you will need is at your fingertips. Starting out can be daunting, but this book's clear, step-by-step instructions will point you in the right direction, and show you the best websites and archives to help you with your research.

Tracing Your Family History Made Easy guides you through the early stages of research, from finding your ancestors in the census and civil registration records – the basic building blocks of any family tree – to other useful records such as parish registers, wills, obituaries, occupational records, school and hospital records, and much more. Later chapters show you how to build your family tree on a PC and share it online, and how the internet can help you make genealogy friends and find living relatives.

There is also a CD-Rom of family tree software, Family Historian Starter Edition 4.1, which enables to you to add up to 80 people per file, create a website and more besides.

Throughout the book you will find all kinds of useful tips, as well as a handy jargon buster at the end to explain some of the terms you will come across in your research. There is also a list of useful websites and some suggestions for further reading.

How you use this book is up to you. If you are completely new to family history you might find it best to start at the beginning and work your way through. Otherwise, you might just want to dip into the chapters that particularly interest you. The index at the back will help pinpoint what you are looking for. So, let's get started!

GETTING STARTED

By reading and following all the steps
in this chapter, you will find out how to:

▶ **Start building up a collection
of useful family documents,
memorabilia and stories**

▶ **Organise your research**

▶ **Start drawing up a family tree**

MAKE A PLAN

Why do you want to research your family history? Is it to create a purely factual record of your ancestry? Or do you want to flesh out your research with stories about your ancestors' lives – their occupations, their hobbies and interests, their personalities and the places they lived in, for example?

People research their family history for all kinds of reasons. They might hope to discover entitlement to a share of land or property, or perhaps whether a diagnosed illness is hereditary, which would have ramifications for their own children. Increasingly, though, people want to find out about their ancestors simply because they are fascinated by their past. Discovering that your ancestor was a war hero, for example, or had royal or aristocratic connections, can be a real thrill.

TIP

Bear in mind that the further back you go, the harder it will be to find relevant records – and those you do track down might be incomplete or difficult to decipher.

Before you embark on what will undoubtedly be an exciting journey of discovery, it is worth taking a few minutes to think about what you want to achieve from your researches. This can help focus your attention, as it's very easy to get sidetracked.

It is also worth thinking about how far back you want to go, and how widely you want to cast your net. Do you want to focus solely on your own family tree, or do you want to include your partner's ancestry as well? Even if you want your research to be as comprehensive as possible, you will find it easier and less daunting to start with a fairly narrow focus, and then gradually expand later on.

Some possible starting points or limitations to your research include:

- ▶ Research just one surname.
- ▶ Focus only on your paternal or maternal ancestry.
- ▶ Go back just two or three generations.
- ▶ If you have a particular area of interest, limit your research to ancestors connected to that subject – ancestors who fought in the two world wars, for example, or were involved in a particular occupation.
- ▶ Focusing on one ancestor only – if you know you have a famous ancestor, or an ancestor who did something remarkable, you might just want to research his/her life.

Next step

For more information about tracing military records and other occupations, see pages 137–40.

START WITH YOURSELF

The best place to start your family history research is with yourself and your immediate family. From there you can gradually work backwards in a logical and systematic way.

1 Start by jotting down essential facts about yourself, including:
- ▶ Your full name and any nicknames.
- ▶ Your date and place of birth.
- ▶ The date and place of your baptism, if applicable.
- ▶ If you were born overseas, the date you came to the UK, and the date you became a UK citizen.
- ▶ Which schools and higher education establishments you attended, with dates.
- ▶ Your occupation(s), again with dates.
- ▶ The name of your spouse or partner, plus the place and date of your marriage/civil ceremony.
- ▶ The names of your immediate family – parents, grandparents, siblings, children (including adopted).
- ▶ Your religious denomination.

TIP

As you make your notes, make a list of the things you want to follow up later.

2 Depending on how detailed you want your research to be, you could add other information such as:
- ▶ Your hobbies and interests, plus any societies/organisations you are (or have been) involved with.
- ▶ Membership of any professional bodies.
- ▶ School/higher education/professional qualifications.
- ▶ If you've ever been in hospital, the name of the hospital(s), the date(s) and the reason(s).
- ▶ Any other interesting facts you can think of about yourself – family histories can be greatly enlivened by interesting or funny stories, which will fascinate and entertain not just your current family but also future generations.

3 Now jot down as much of the above information as you can for immediate members of the family – including, where relevant, dates of death and places of burial. Don't worry at this stage if there are gaps in your knowledge; the main purpose here is to highlight what you do know, then you can set about researching the facts you don't know. Any missing details can be indicated with a question mark, so that you can quickly identify further areas of research.

MAKE USE OF FAMILY MEMORABILIA

Gather together as much family paperwork and other memorabilia as you can, as they can all help to piece together the family jigsaw, as well as giving fascinating insights into your ancestors' lives. Useful items include:

- ▶ Letters and postcards.
- ▶ Diaries.
- ▶ School/college/university records/reports.
- ▶ Professional certificates.
- ▶ Military records and memorabilia (including war medals).
- ▶ War memorabilia, such as recipes and ration books.
- ▶ Birth, marriage and death certificates (finding these will save you money, as you have to pay for copies from the General Registry Office or local Record Office).
- ▶ Birthday and address books.
- ▶ Greetings/congratulations cards.
- ▶ Invitations to weddings, christenings or other family events.
- ▶ Books with personal messages handwritten inside.
- ▶ Newspaper cuttings (which could cover anything from the time a relative appeared in a local panto to an obituary).
- ▶ Pension books.
- ▶ House deeds.
- ▶ Copies of wills.
- ▶ Passports.
- ▶ Business ledgers (which may have notes in the margins).
- ▶ Home videos (such as weddings), tape recordings and oral histories.

TIP

People don't always record details accurately, so make sure you verify all facts later on. A forgetful grandparent, for example, could easily write the wrong date onto the flyleaf of a book.

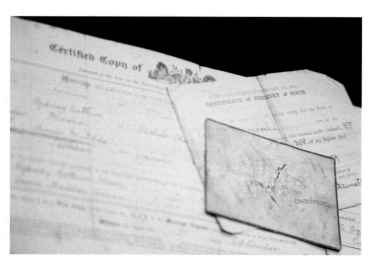

Some of these will obviously be easier to get hold of than others. Don't worry if you can't find any of the above, there are plenty of other ways of finding out about your ancestors. Pages 26–46 will show you how to find out more through censuses and the Births, Marriages and Deaths (BMD) Index.

Photographs

These are particularly useful for the family historian, as they can tell you a lot about your ancestors. Dates, places and the identities of those pictured will hopefully be written on the back. If not, you'll have to turn detective. Looking at the clothing might help to pinpoint the era, while uniforms will indicate an occupation (such as nursing) or military regiment.

Wedding pictures and other large family groups can often help identify several people at once, and perhaps even include people you didn't know existed – suggesting, perhaps, that some of those pictured were close family friends or relatives who died young. These will be interesting avenues to explore later.

The family bible

Popular with the Victorians, family bibles are now increasingly rare, but if you are lucky enough to unearth one among your memorabilia, you could find all kinds of useful information within its pages.

Victorian family bibles were not just used for spiritual and educational purposes; they also served as a repository for family records. Family trees were often written onto the inside front cover and flyleaf, along with details about births, baptisms, marriages and deaths. Sometimes even the deaths of pets were recorded.

Other useful documents, such as newspaper cuttings, photographs, letters and birthday cards, often found their way into the family bible, tucked into its pages for safe keeping.

Jargon buster

Repository
Any library, archive or record office that holds family history records.

TALK TO FAMILY MEMBERS

Once you've gathered as much information and memorabilia as you can, the next step is to talk to members of your family. Older relatives are a particularly fruitful source of family knowledge, and can often help to identify people in photographs or fill in gaps such as birth details or occupations. They will also have a treasure trove of fascinating stories to pass on.

This is where you might discover:
▶ Relatives' religious beliefs and political allegiances.
▶ Where they went on holiday.
▶ What their interests were.
▶ What sort of jobs they had.
▶ Perhaps even a family rift or scandal.

Jargon buster ▶

Primary source
Original document, such as a birth, marriage or death certificate.

All of this helps to bring your family history to life, and turns those names on documents into real people. You might find, for instance, that you have a lot in common with your great-grandmother, and this can give you a genuine feeling of connection.

Organise your time

Make it a priority to talk to your oldest relatives while they are still around, before some facts and stories get lost forever. They could be the only ones who can identify someone in a photograph, for example, or the only ones with access to certain facts and anecdotes. But talking to younger relatives can be fruitful, too – they may have obtained details and stories from deceased relatives, hold useful documents, or have perhaps started a family tree themselves, in which case you can share information that you have discovered.

It is usually best to interview just one relative at a time, so that you can focus on what that person has to say. But sometimes group interviews can be good too, as something that one person says might spark off a memory with someone else.

GET THE MOST OUT OF YOUR INTERVIEW

Preparation is key. Make a list of topics that you want to cover, and try to arrange them chronologically – people often remember things better if taken through events in chronological order.

Gather together any memorabilia you think may be useful to take along. Photos, for example, can help jog people's memories, and they might also be able to supply missing details such as the identities of people in the picture, the date, the place, the occasion and even the story behind the picture.

Possible topics for interviews

Much of the information you gathered about yourself will be useful in relation to members of your family, so you could use the list on page 9 as a starting point. Other possible topics include:

▶ Details of other members of the family, such as their parents and grandparents.

▶ Contact details for living relatives, so that you can get in touch with them.

▶ Any photos, documents and other memorabilia that they would be willing to give or lend to you.

▶ Any family research they have done themselves. With the increasing popularity of family history research, it's likely that other family members will have started tracing their family tree and will be happy to share their findings with you.

▶ Interesting stories about their lives. For older relatives this could include what their childhood was like, the clothes they wore, the food they ate, the games they played, what they did at school, what it was like living in wartime Britain, and much more.

Essential equipment

Take with you a notebook and pen (plus two or three spares, just in case!). Some kind of recording device, such as a digital voice recorder, a camcorder or a camera with videoing facility, can be very helpful, too. Remember, however, that if you are using a battery-operated recording device, you need to take spare batteries.

TIP
Try to find out family nicknames. The names family members were known as may not be the same as the name that appears on a birth, marriage or death certificate.

BE CAREFUL

Bear in mind that your relations, especially older ones, may not remember things correctly. You may also find that different members of your family have different recollections of events. So always treat information with caution, and check facts against primary sources.

Interview dos and don'ts

Do:

▶ Be flexible – if people wander off the point, let them talk as they might volunteer other useful information. Then gently guide them back to the original topic.

▶ Be patient – older people can take a while to answer questions, so don't be tempted to rush them. There is no need to rush to fill silences.

▶ Be prepared to deviate from your list of topics – some of the answers given might suggest other questions.

▶ Listen carefully – it doesn't look good to ask about something already covered.

▶ Ask short, simple questions, rather than long complicated ones.

▶ Keep the interview fairly short. Older people tire easily, so you might need to interview them over several visits. An hour at a time is usually plenty.

▶ Thank your interviewee. It may seem obvious, but it will be remembered and appreciated, and will stand you in good stead if you need more information.

Don't:

▶ Ask questions that could elicit 'Yes' or 'No' answers. So instead of 'Did you get on well with your parents?', you could ask, 'How well did you get on with your parents?' or 'What was your relationship with your parents like?'

▶ Ask leading questions, such as 'Did you hate having to leave school at 14?' Instead, ask: 'How did you feel about leaving school at 14?'

▶ Interrupt – not only is it discourteous, you might find that you have missed something interesting!

▶ Talk too much – let your interviewee do the talking.

▶ Try to force an issue if your relative appears reluctant or embarrassed about answering something. Remember that things such as illegitimacy were not as acceptable two or three generations ago as they are now.

After the interview

▶ Jot down any particular points of interest or things you want to follow up while the interview is still fresh in your memory.

▶ Transcribing is hard work so it's tempting to put it off. Try to make yourself sit down and make a start as soon as possible, but limit yourself to about 40 minutes to an hour at a time to stay fresh.

- As you transcribe, jot down any pieces of information that are unclear on the recording so that you can verify facts at a later date.
- Jot down any other questions that occur to you for a follow-up interview.
- Don't be tempted to tidy up a person's narrative too much. Leave in grammatical errors, colloquialisms and local dialect as they are all part of that person's character.
- Once you have transcribed the interview, print it out so that you can refer to it easily, but it's useful to store it electronically as well, perhaps in a dedicated folder on your computer.

Email interviews

Sometimes it is difficult to interview in person, perhaps because your relation is hard of hearing or lives too far away. As long as your relation is computer savvy – and increasing numbers of older people these days are – then an email interview is a good substitute. It also means you avoid hours of transcribing oral interviews, as you have a ready-made transcription. The disadvantage is that you may not capture the same sense of a person's character, as people tend to be more formal when typing than they are when speaking.

Use interviews to fill in your family tree

Now might be a good time to start drawing up a family tree, as your interviews might well yield useful names and dates. Pages 16–19 talk you through the process of getting started.

Perhaps, for example, you've been talking to Great Uncle George, and he was able to tell you the date he was married, and possibly the birth, marriage and death dates of his parents or other members of his family. Perhaps he also had copies of their certificates, which verified their full names and relevant dates.

Sometimes talking to a family member can throw up details of someone you didn't know existed. Maybe your grandmother had a brother who became estranged from some members of the family. But Great Uncle George might have kept in touch with him, and be able to tell you all about him. Now you have a new person to add to your family tree, hopefully with dates as well.

Even if relatives are unsure of certain details, the information they can give you might open up useful leads. Perhaps Great Uncle John can only find his parents' marriage and death certificates, but there should be enough information on these for you to be able to track down their birth certificates as well. Pages 26–46 go into this in more detail.

KEEPING RECORDS

Start keeping records straightaway, as they could save you hours of wasted time later on. As your research progresses, you will gradually develop a system that suits you, but here are a few ideas and a sample record page showing how you could record your research.

JONES, MICHAEL WILLIAM	J11
Date of birth:	22nd April 1908
Place of birth:	Blackburn, Lancashire
Father:	George Arthur JONES (J09)
Mother:	Mary Elizabeth HEATH (H01)
Spouse:	Alice Rosemary BROWN (B01)
Married:	24th August 1931
Place of marriage:	Wimbledon, London SW1
Occupation:	Teacher
Siblings:	George Henry JONES, b. 29/7/1906 (J10) Elizabeth Margaret JONES (later WILSON), b. 4/5/1910 (J12) Victoria Alice JONES (later GREEN), b. 6/10/1912 (J13) Samuel Edward JONES, b. 9/3/1913 (J14)
Issue:	Michael George JONES, b. 8/11/32 (J15) Matilda Mary JONES (later SEYMOUR), b. 12/7/36 (J16)
Died:	15th September 1963; Coalville, Leicestershire
Cause:	Heart attack
Buried:	Coalville, Leicestershire

Documents consulted:
Birth certificate (copy obtained 3/11/10)
Marriage certificate (copy obtained 7/11/10)
Death certificate (copy obtained 24/11/10)

Other sources:
Spoke to Lydia Mary Jones (granddaughter – daughter of Michael George Jones J15) on 4/9/10 – confirmed some of above details, and gave personal memories (transcript attached – original recording on tape 012)

Notes:
Still to do – search census returns to confirm addresses – when moved from Blackburn to Coalville? And why?
Check BMD for siblings, spouse and children
Last update: 24/11/10

▶ Although you will probably want to store information on your computer, it is also useful to have printouts for easy reference. This is also a good safety back-up in case of computer failure.

▶ An A4 or foolscap lever-arch file is ideal for storing your notes, along with any family papers you find.

▶ Make up a record page for each person in your family, so that you can add or update details as you go along. It is a good idea to give each family member a unique identification number, as this will prevent confusion if you have people with the same or similar names. It is also useful when cross-referencing from one record page to another (see the sample on the left).

▶ Keep notes of the source of each piece of information, and the date you obtained it, so that you can check back later on if necessary.

▶ Keep details of everyone you speak to or write to – you may need to contact them again.

▶ Record negative results as well as the positive ones, so that you don't needlessly go back over old ground. For example: Mabel BROWN, buried at Anytown Cemetery, according to Uncle John; visited 12/4/10; no trace.

START YOUR FAMILY TREE

It's a good idea to start drawing up a simple family tree as soon as possible. Then, at a glance, you can see people's names, relevant dates and how they are related to each other. You can also easily see where there are gaps in your knowledge, and this will help you formulate a plan of action.

There are a variety of software packages available to help you build your family tree, and these have a number of advantages, including making it easy to update, share online and add other features such as photographs and video/audio clips. Pages 172–81 talks you through this in more detail, but to begin with you might find it easiest to draw up a family tree on paper.

Start with a drop-line chart

The most common format is the drop-line chart, which is clear and simple to create and use (see overleaf). You can either draw a chart by hand, type one up on a computer, or use a CD-Rom application such as Tree Draw or Gen Designer. Start with a good-sized sheet of paper – A3 is ideal – so that you have space for plenty of names. Later on you can simply add more sheets of paper as the tree expands.

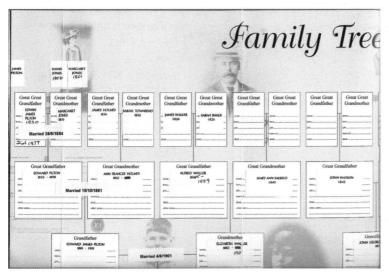

If you want to be a bit more artistic, there are some more fancy ways of presenting your family tree. Romans displayed their family pedigrees on tree-like charts – hence the term 'family tree' – and these remained popular right up to the Victorian era. They are an attractive format if you are limiting your research to two or three generations, but are not really practicable if you are hoping to make your research as comprehensive as possible.

TIP
If you have room, pin your family tree up on a wall so that it's constantly handy.

Next step
You can also build your family tree on your computer: see pages 174–85.

Jargon buster

Pedigree chart
A vertical chart that records direct ascendants and descendants only. It can be useful to start with a pedigree chart, and gradually expand into a drop-line chart, which spreads in all directions.

CREATE A DROP-LINE CHART

To create a simple drop-line chart, you just need paper, pen or pencil and a ruler. You might find it useful to draw up a rough chart to begin with, and then make a neat copy afterwards. If you don't want to draw up your chart yourself, you can buy templates from newsagents or genealogy specialists, such as S&N Genealogy suppliers (see Useful Addresses, page 218).

If anyone has married more than once, display the marriages in chronological order, left to right.

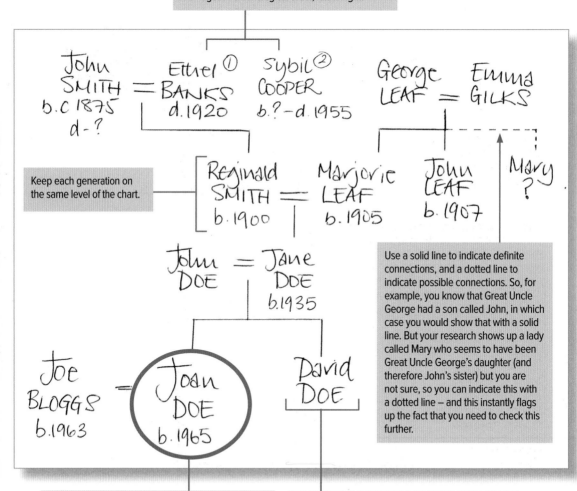

Keep each generation on the same level of the chart.

Use a solid line to indicate definite connections, and a dotted line to indicate possible connections. So, for example, you know that Great Uncle George had a son called John, in which case you would show that with a solid line. But your research shows up a lady called Mary who seems to have been Great Uncle George's daughter (and therefore John's sister) but you are not sure, so you can indicate this with a dotted line – and this instantly flags up the fact that you need to check this further.

Start with your own name, then work upwards, adding parents, grandparents, great-grandparents, etc. Then work outwards and downwards, adding partner, siblings and children, uncles and aunts, cousins, etc.

Surnames are usually put in upper case, forenames in lower case. If you look at earlier family trees, you may find that men's surnames are included but not those of women.

As you add each person, enter as many known basic details as you know at this stage – forename(s) and surname, with dates and places of birth and/or baptism, marriage and death

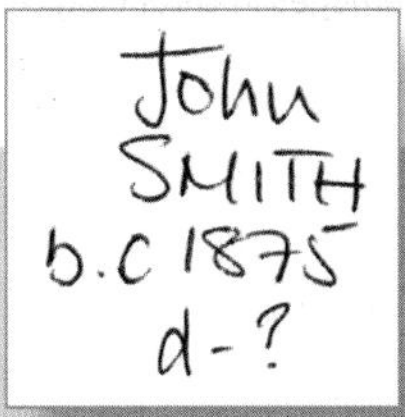

John
SMITH
b.C 1875
d - ?

TIP
See page 24 for a list of common abbreviations to help you record information quickly.

When putting details of a married couple, it is conventional to put men on the left and women on the right.

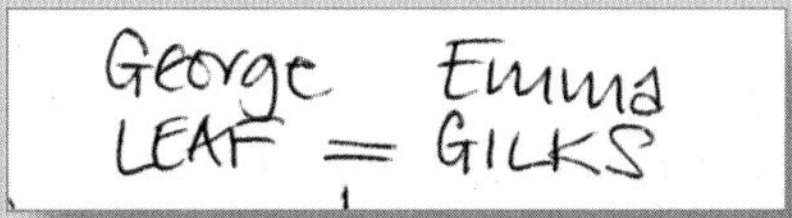

George   Emma
LEAF = GILKS

Indicate gaps in your research with a question mark; this will make it easier for you to spot areas that you still need to research. Similarly, for any details that you are uncertain about, enter but follow with a question mark – for example, d. 4th July (?) 1849 – or just put c.1850 if you only have an approximate idea. It at least gives you something to go on.

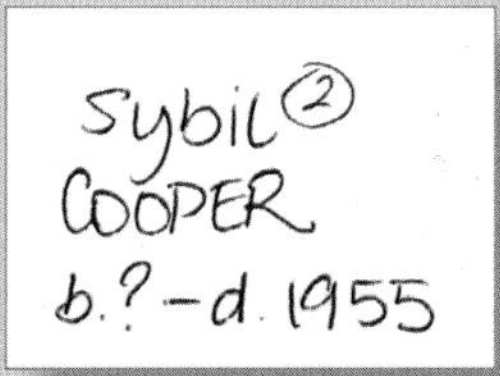

Sybil ②
COOPER
b. ? - d. 1955

Children are usually displayed in order of birth (not, as used to be the case, all the boys first, then the girls), and should be shown descending from both parents, not just the father or the mother.

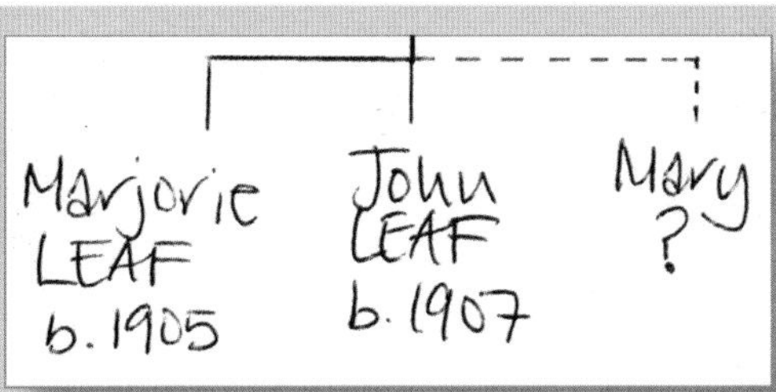

Marjorie
LEAF
b. 1905

John
LEAF
b. 1907

Mary
?

Enter as much as you can from the information you have gathered so far from your various sources, such as family memorabilia and interviews. Later on in your research, when perhaps you have visited libraries or record offices or done some online searching, you can add more details.

FIND OTHER LIVING RELATIVES

With the advent of the internet, researching your family tree has never been easier, and one way in which it can be invaluable is for tracking down living relatives that you might not know exist.

Genealogy websites

There are a number of genealogy websites where you can find details of people researching the same topics as you, make contact with them and hopefully share information.

Next step ▶

For more information about web forums, see pages 196–8.

A good site to start with is http://genforum.genealogy.com, where you can search for ancestors by surname, region or other topics such as religious denomination or occupation, any of which will give you access to a relevant genealogy forum. You can then click on any of the people listed to find out more about them, post follow-up messages and find out the email address of people who have posted messages to the forum. Unlike many similar sites, access is free.

Search for relatives online

Suppose, for example, you want to search for the surname Parker and you think your family has always been based in the United Kingdom, you would:

1 Go to **http://genforum.genealogy.com**. You can search using the 'Forum Finder' or 'Surnames' buttons, but as this site covers the whole world it is best to click **Countries** under the 'Regional' heading

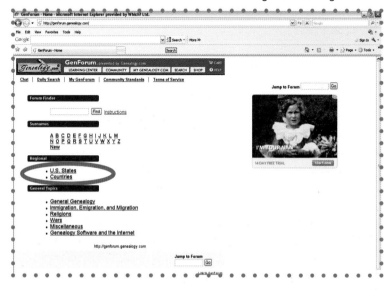

2 Click **United Kingdom** and then **Go**

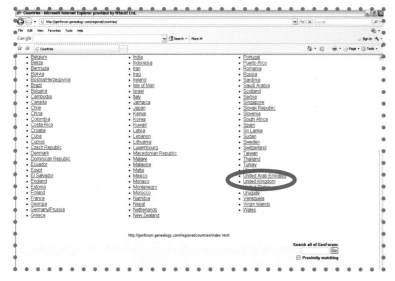

3 Enter 'Parker' in the 'Search this forum' box and click **Go**. A list of results will be displayed – in this case, as this is a fairly common surname, there are 388 matches. These have all been posted by people sharing information about family members and requesting further details

4 Scroll down to see if any might relate to your branch of the family. Some entries give additional details at this stage, such as birth dates, names of spouses, place of birth or later residence. This can help to identify people related to you and you can weed out those unlikely to be of interest

▶ Getting Started

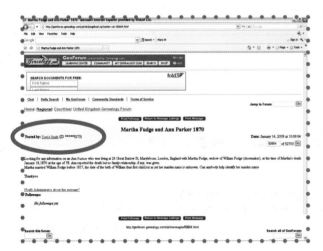

5 If you find an entry that interests you, click on it and see what comes up. Let's suppose, for example, that you are interested in Martha Fudge and Ann Parker. If you click on that entry, quite a bit of information comes up

6 If you know that Ann Parker is an ancestor of yours, or looks as though she might be, you can get in touch with the person who posted the message by clicking on the name. The next screen will display their email address

7 If you can supply any of the requested information, click **Post Followup** at the bottom of the screen. There is also a 'Print message' button if you want to keep a copy for your records

8 If you can't find any Parkers connected to you, try searching again using a different surname. For example, if Parker was your maternal grandfather's name, you could try your grandmother's maiden name instead, especially if it is a less common surname

Other websites
Other websites worth looking at when searching for a relative online include:
www.curiousfox.com
www.genesreunited.co.uk
http://lists.rootsweb.com
http://boards.ancestry.com
www.ancestry.myfamily.com
http://worldconnect.genealogy.rootsweb.com

Note, though, that for most of these you will need to pay a subscription to gain full access to information and records.

Use telephone directories
Telephone directories can also be a good way of tracking down relatives, but only if you have a fairly unusual surname – if you are called Jones or Smith, this might not be the best way forward for you! Directories covering the whole country should be available in your local library.

Alternatively, there are a number of online telephone directories, which allow you to search for people even if you have only

approximate details or spellings. The most comprehensive site is www.192. com (see above), which allows you to search for people, businesses and places, as well as electoral rolls and births and marriages. Searches are free.

Another useful online directory is the official BT site, www.btexchanges.com, which is essentially the same information as that found in the printed regional directories, and it is regularly updated. The same site also offers a postcode look-up service, which could be useful if you know which area you want to search. To use the site you need to register, but registration is free.

If you want to find relatives overseas, you might find www.infobel.com/en/uk useful – it covers businesses and individuals all over the world.

Use family history societies

Another way of getting help with tracking down relatives, both living and deceased, is to join a family history society. The facilities offered varies from one society to another, but most hold regular meetings, publish journals and booklets, run family history courses, carry out various family history projects (such as transcribing and indexing documents) and have forums where members can exchange information. Most also have very useful websites.

Your own local family history society will be useful, but you might also find it helpful to join the society for whichever region your ancestor came from.

Contacting relatives

Once you have discovered the names of people who might be related to you, it is best to write or email, rather than phone; people might not take kindly to being phoned out of the blue, especially if it turns out they are not related to you! If you write, always enclose a stamped addressed envelope – not only is it a courtesy to them, but it might make them feel more inclined to reply.

TIP
Note where people with a particular surname are living – you may notice that a large number live in a specific area, for example. This is a good indication of where people with the same surname were living 100 or more years ago.

FAMILY TREE ABBREVIATIONS

Family trees use a set of conventional symbols and abbreviations, which will be useful both for drawing up your own family tree and for interpreting others you may come across in your research. Here are some common and more unusual abbreviations you may come across.

b.	Born
bach.	Bachelor
bp. or bpt.	Baptised
bur.	Buried
c.	Circa, or about
coh.	Coheir(ess)
Diss.	Marriage dissolved/divorce
d.	Died
dsp	Died without issue
dvp	Died before father
d.yng.	Died young
ed.	Educated
fl.	Lived
inft	Infant
kia	Killed in action
mar.	Marriage
MI	Memorial Inscription (indicates existence of gravestone or other memorial – see pages 167–8)
miw	Mentioned in will of...
Ob./Obit.	Died (less common than d.)
= or m.	Married
spin.	Spinster
unm.	Unmarried
w.pr.	Will proved

THE CENSUS EXPLAINED

By reading and following all the steps
in this chapter, you will find out:

▶ **What the census is and how it can
help your family history research**

▶ **How to use census indexes**

▶ **How to read and interpret a census
document**

KNOW THE CENSUS HISTORY

National censuses began in Britain in 1801 to try to assess the growth of the population and its make-up in terms of age, gender and occupation. They have been taken at regular ten-year intervals ever since, apart from in 1941.

Each census records details of every person in a household on a specific night, from family members down to servants. It is worth bearing in mind that they were not designed to aid family historians, but to enable social and financial planning and, during wartime, how many men were available to call up. So although the later censuses, in particular, are very detailed, they are not always accurate and facts gleaned from them should be checked against other sources. Nevertheless, they give us a fascinating glimpse into our ancestors' lives, and can help to confirm family links.

The earliest censuses were carried out by parish officials in England and Wales, and by schoolmasters in Scotland, but few of these survive. From 1841, the census was in the hands of the General Register Office (GRO), and from that point onwards they become increasingly detailed.

The collection of census information was organised into the same districts and sub-districts used for civil registration (see pages 48–72), with the sub-districts further divided into enumeration districts.

Each census worked by having paid enumerators distributing census forms (known as 'schedules') to every household within their enumeration district and returning after census night to collect the completed forms. They then entered the information from the forms into enumerators' books. In most cases, the original forms were later destroyed, so it is the enumerators' books that are available for research. The exception is the 1911 census, for which householder schedules have survived.

Censuses only become available for public viewing after 100 years, so the 1911 census has recently been released.

Jargon buster

General Register Office (GRO)
The Government department responsible for the registration of births, marriages and deaths from 1837, and for the censuses from 1841.

The Census Explained

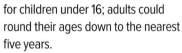

BE CAREFUL

People filling in the census returns often estimated answers or didn't fully understand the questions; in addition, enumerators often made mistakes when transferring material. So information contained in the census isn't 100 per cent reliable.

WHAT CAN THE CENSUS TELL YOU?

Information that you can glean from the censuses includes:

▶ Where people were living on the census night, even if this was not their usual address.

▶ Full names of all occupants.

▶ From 1851, occupants' relationship to the head of the household (usually the senior male).

▶ Gender.

▶ Marital status.

▶ Rank, profession or occupation, including, from 1891, whether they were employed, self-employed or unemployed. More details about occupation and employment status were included from the 1911 census onwards.

▶ Age – although note that in the 1841 census, exact ages were only required for children under 16; adults could round their ages down to the nearest five years.

▶ Place of birth. In the 1841 census people were required only to state their county of birth, but from the 1851 census onwards the parish was also included.

▶ Whether any members of the household were born overseas.

▶ From 1851, whether any members of the household were deaf, dumb, blind or lunatic.

▶ In 1891, census returns for Wales and Monmouthshire asked whether householders could speak English, Welsh or both languages.

▶ From 1911, women had to state how many years they had been married, the number of children born alive and the number still living.

WHERE TO FIND THE CENSUSES

Once available only on microfilm/fiche at places such as The National Archives and county record offices, the enumerators' pages from the census returns for 1841 to 1911 are now also available to view online, having been fully transcribed and indexed. You can usually view the indexes free, for example at www.familysearch.org or www.ancestry.co.uk, but you will then need to pay to look at a transcript or original document. In addition, microfilm/fiche copies are still available at most local libraries and record offices, and there is a complete set at The National Archives.

Search on www.familysearch.org

Each census from 1841 to 1911 has been transcribed and indexed by the Church of Jesus Christ of Latter-Day Saints (Mormons). The most detailed of the earlier indexes is for the 1881 census and includes almost as much information as you would expect to find on the original documents. The indexes are available to view free of charge at www.familysearch.org.

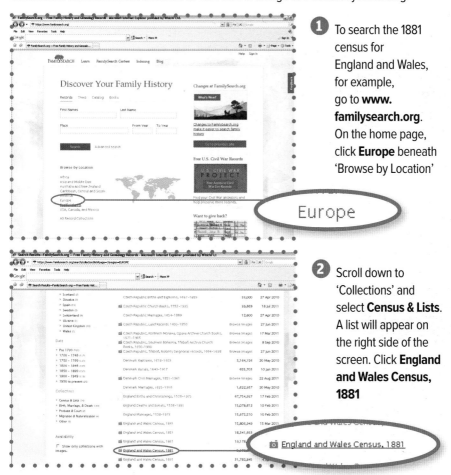

1 To search the 1881 census for England and Wales, for example, go to **www.familysearch.org**. On the home page, click **Europe** beneath 'Browse by Location'

2 Scroll down to 'Collections' and select **Census & Lists**. A list will appear on the right side of the screen. Click **England and Wales Census, 1881**

England and Wales Census, 1881

Description
Population schedule for England, Wales, Isle of Man and Channel Islands showing population as of 3 April 1881.

Learn more »

Search Collection
First Names   Last Name

Place   From Year   To Year

Search   — Advanced search

Learn   Family Search Centers   Indexing   Blog

England and Wales Census, 1881
Search all collections
1–20 of 8,869 results for >Name: **Joshua Smithson**

Try adding more search terms to improve your search results.

Joshua E Smithson
England and Wales Census, 1881
birth: 1859 —Kirkdale, Lancashire, England
residence: 1881 —Kirkdale, Lancashire, England
census: 1881 —Kirkdale, Lancashire, England
parents: Emma Smithson

Joshua Smithson
England and Wales Census, 1881
birth: 1869 —Ossett, Yorkshire, England
residence: 1881 —Hunslet, Yorkshire (West Riding), England
census: 1881 —Hunslet, Yorkshire (West Riding), England
parents: George Smithson, Emma Smithson

Joshua Smithson
England and Wales Census, 1881
birth: 1818 —Preston Patrick, Westmorland, England
residence: 1881 —Hipperholme With Brighouse, Yorkshire (West Riding), England

3 Enter as many known details about your ancestor as you can into the box that appears on the screen. The more facts you know, the more it will narrow down your search

4 For example, a search for a Joshua Smithson, yielded thousands of results

5 This is clearly a lot of records to search, so it would be worth going back to the data entry screen and entering more known details if you have any. If not, you will have to scroll through the results until you find one that looks as though it could be your ancestor. You can help to decide this by other facts given on the results page – such as date of birth, residence at the time of the census and names of parents

6 Suppose the first Joshua Smithson on the list looked a likely match. Click the down arrow to the right of his details to see a preview

7 This brings up all details from the census return, including Joshua Smithson's age, his marital status, occupation, full address of his place of residence on census night, and where to find the original record

8 These extra factors will hopefully help you decide whether this is indeed your ancestor. Sometimes, as in this record, there is only a mother listed and no father, which cuts down the known factors that you can check against

England and Wales Census, 1881
Search all collections
1–20 of 8,869 results for >Name: **Joshua Smithson**

Try adding more search terms to improve your search results.

Joshua E Smithson
England and Wales Census, 1881
birth: 1859 —Kirkdale, Lancashire, England
residence: 1881 —Kirkdale, Lancashire, England
census: 1881 —Kirkdale, Lancashire,
parents: Emma Smithson
record title: England and Wales Census, 1881
name: Joshua E Smithson
age: 22
gender: Male
birth year: 1859
birthplace: Kirkdale, Lancashire, England
relationship to head of household: Son
marital condition: Single
profession/occupation: Watchmaker Finisher
address: 85 St Johns Rd
census place: Kirkdale, Lancashire, England

Make checks

It is always worth making a few further checks to ensure you are on the right path and finding information about the right relative. For example:

1 You could try finding out more about Emma Smithson by returning to the home page and entering what you know about her – you know her full residential address and that she had a son. The list of results is headed by an Emma Smithson with a son called Joshua E. Smithson, with the same place of residence, so this looks a likely match

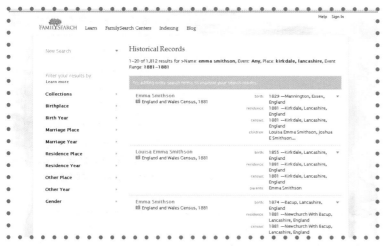

2 As before, click the down arrow to bring up more details about Emma Smithson. Now you can see that she was a widow rather than an unmarried mother (therefore Smithson is her married name, not her maiden name), and it gives her age, birth year, birthplace, occupation and names of other children

3 Now search for Emma Smithson and Joshua E. Smithson again in previous and later census returns, following exactly the same procedure. This will help you to piece together their lives, and hopefully enable you to decide at some stage whether these are indeed your ancestors or not

4 Once you are reasonably certain that these are your ancestors, you can also find out more about Emma and Joshua E. Smithson (and the other children listed at the same household on census night) through civil registration records (see pages 48–72). You can also see from your search results where to view the original census returns at The National Archives (see page 33)

Other websites for index searches

You can do searches and view transcripts free of charge at www.freecen.org. uk/, but currently it only covers 1841–91.

Free index searches are available on a number of other websites, including:

www.ancestry.co.uk (see pages 34–5)

www.findmypast.co.uk

www.genesreunited.com

www.thegenealogist.co.uk

www.britishorigins.com (1841, 1861 and 1871 only)

The 1911 census has its own website: www.1911census.co.uk.

For all of these, you will need to pay to view original documents or transcriptions (see page 46).

Census dates and National Archives reference numbers

You can also access information at The National Archives, too (see pages 108–14). Documents at The National Archives are grouped under reference numbers and the relevant ones for the censuses are as follows:

Census	Date taken	Reference number
1841	6 June	HO 107
1851	30 March	HO 107
1861	7 April	RG 9
1871	2 April	RG 10
1881	3 April	RG 11
1891	5 April	RG 12
1901	31 March	RG 13
1911	2 April	RG 14

However, as with other websites that have free index searches (see opposite), when it comes to viewing the original documents, The National Archives works with partner websites for which you have to pay to access the documents. For the census returns of 1841 to 1891, this is www.ancestry.co.uk (see pages 34–5), for 1901 it is www.1901censusonline.com in assocation with Genes Reunited and for 1911 it is www.1911census.co.uk.

Jargon buster

The National Archives
The National Archives at Kew in Surrey is the UK's principal repository for the United Kingdom, containing over 11 million documents from the 11th century to the present. Records can be viewed at Kew, either in their original form or on microfilm/fiche, plus many are available online.

the census explained

The Census Explained

TRY THIS

If you plan to print your census records you can save ink by cropping the black border in your picture-editing software. If it has a Text tool, add a note to make it easy to see who the page refers to and the census year. Otherwise it is easy to confuse sheets from different censuses as they look similar.

DOWNLOAD A CENSUS RECORD

As with www.familysearch.org, you can search the census indexes online at www.ancestry.co.uk, but in addition you can download census records on this website if you pay a subscription or purchase vouchers (see page 46). Here's how to locate and download a census record.

1 Go to **www.ancestry.co.uk**. The home page lists the records available on the website as well as offering general searches. Searching all the records can produce so many results, especially for common names, that you are often better concentrating on a specific record, such as a census

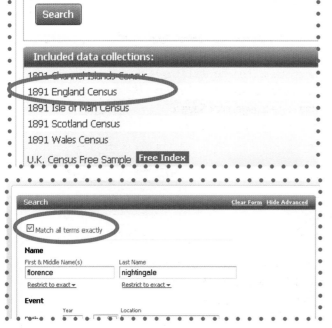

2 Click **Search** in the top menu bar, then **Census & Electoral Roll**. Click on a census, in this case **1891 UK Census Collection** from the list on the right. Scroll to the bottom of the page and click **1891 England Census**

3 Enter as much information as you have into the search boxes. Tick the 'Match all terms exactly' box to hopefully home straight in on the person you want. You can always relax the criteria later if your initial search fails

4 The results of your search lists brief details about people who match your criteria, though you can see more details by clicking **View Record** to the left of the person's name. If the information displayed looks promising, click **View original image**

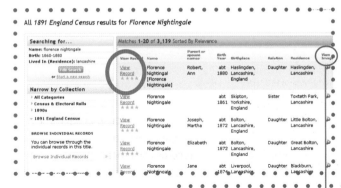

5 If your initial search fails to locate your ancestor, return to the search page to broaden your criteria. Click the arrow next to 'Restrict to exact'. First try including 'Phonetic matches'. This analyses names phonetically and matches them to others that sound similar but are spelled differently, such as Page and Paige. Many people in the 19th century were illiterate, so the census enumerators recorded names as they heard them

6 If you still can't find the person you want, uncheck the 'Match all terms exactly' box. The results will now include individuals matching your search criteria to varying degrees. These results are given a star rating based on how close they are to your initial facts

7 Once you have a record you want to view, clicking the **View Image** icon on the right of the search results gives you the option to view a picture of the page from the census enumerator's book. The zoom tool enables you to magnify the page and check that the written details are for your ancestor. When you are satisfied it is the correct page, click **Save** to download a copy you can refer to at a later stage in your research

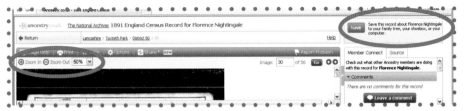

8 Pick the 'Save this image' option to save a copy to your computer's hard drive. Right-click on the image and select **Save Picture as** from the list of options that appears. Navigate to your chosen folder, give the file a suitable name, and click **Save** to store it in JPEG format

BE CAREFUL

Don't assume that someone from the past who shares your surname must be your ancestor, even if you have a really unusual name.

EXPLORE DIFFERENT CENSUSES

By delving into different censuses you can start fleshing out details relating to your ancestors. For example:

1 Go to **www.familysearch.org** and, using Joshua E. Smithson once again (see pages 29–31), start a new search, this time starting with the 1911 census. The results show two Joshua E. Smithsons, both living in Lancashire

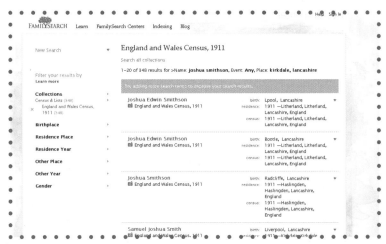

TIP

You can search and view transcripts free of charge at www. freecen.org.uk, but currently it only covers 1841–91.

2 Click the down arrow of both records and it quickly becomes clear that it is the first Joshua E. Smithson we are interested in. If the one we were looking at before was 22 at the time of the 1881 census, then he would have been 52 at the 1911 census. He certainly couldn't have been the second Joshua Smithson listed, as he was only 23 in 1911. The 23-year-old Joshua could, however, have been the 52-year-old Joshua's son, although this is not made clear so you can't assume this to be the case – you will have to check in earlier census records, as well as civil registration records (see pages 48–72)

3 Now you have more information about Joshua – for example, you now know that his middle name is Edwin (it was only listed as an initial in the 1881 census), and that by 1911 he had moved to another part of Lancashire – you can verify this by moving backwards to the 1901 census

4 Return to the Historical Collections page, select the 1901 census and enter known details. This time you can enter both of his forenames in the data form. Once again, you have two Joshua Smithsons – it is fairly clear that they are the same ones you discovered before, as both are ten years younger than in the previous census. Again, it is not clear whether they are father and son, but

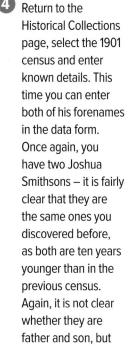

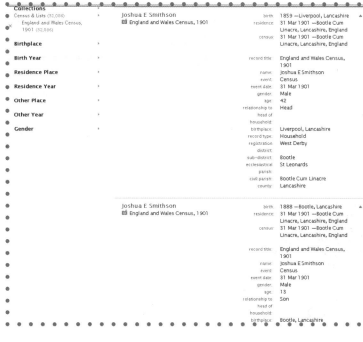

Collections		
Census & Lists (32,086)		
England and Wales Census, 1901 (32,086)		
Birthplace		
Birth Year		
Residence Place		
Residence Year		
Other Place		
Other Year		
Gender		

Joshua E Smithson
England and Wales Census, 1901

birth:	1859 —Liverpool, Lancashire
residence:	31 Mar 1901 —Bootle Cum Linacre, Lancashire, England
census:	31 Mar 1901 —Bootle Cum Linacre, Lancashire, England
record title:	England and Wales Census, 1901
name:	Joshua E Smithson
event:	Census
event date:	31 Mar 1901
gender:	Male
age:	42
relationship to head of household:	Head
birthplace:	Liverpool, Lancashire
record type:	Household
registration district:	West Derby
sub-district:	Bootle
ecclesiastical parish:	St Leonards
civil parish:	Bootle Cum Linacre
county:	Lancashire

Joshua E Smithson
England and Wales Census, 1901

birth:	1888 —Bootle, Lancashire
residence:	31 Mar 1901 —Bootle Cum Linacre, Lancashire, England
census:	31 Mar 1901 —Bootle Cum Linacre, Lancashire, England
record title:	England and Wales Census, 1901
name:	Joshua E Smithson
event:	Census
event date:	31 Mar 1901
gender:	Male
age:	13
relationship to head of household:	Son
birthplace:	Bootle, Lancashire

you can certainly bear the possibility in mind

5 Follow the same procedure for every census, gradually tracing your ancestor and his closest relatives back through the decades. Each census should tell you something different about your ancestors

6 The further back you go, the more family names you will find, so make sure you keep detailed records as you go

7 By the time you have finished searching, you should have more details to add into your family tree. You might well have discovered some ancestors you didn't know existed. For example, you knew that your grandfather had six brothers, but you didn't know that he also had two sisters who died in infancy. As long as those sisters were alive for at least one of the censuses, you should have some useful details about them that you can add to your family tree

Next step

Because the censuses aren't wholly reliable, you will need to verify all information against official registration documents. These are covered in detail on pages 48–72.

CENSUS RETURNS IN SCOTLAND

Scottish census returns tended to be more detailed than the English and Welsh equivalents, with more information about the buildings themselves as well as their occupants. Indexes to Scottish censuses and sample census pages can be viewed at www.scotlandspeople.gov.uk.

CENSUS RETURNS IN IRELAND

Searching Irish records is more problematical; the Irish Public Record Office in Dublin was destroyed by protestors in 1922 and few records survived. However, the 1901 and 1911 censuses are available, and you can view transcripts online, free of charge, at www.census.nationalarchives.ie.

The undermentioned Houses are situate within the Boundaries of the

Civil Parish [or Township] of	City or Municipal Borough of	Municipal Ward of	Parliamentary Borough of	Town or Village or Hamlet of	Urban Sanitary District of
Eastbourne				Eastbourne	Eastbourne

No. of Schedule	ROAD, STREET, &c., and No. or NAME of HOUSE	HOUSES Inhabited	HOUSES Un-inhabited (U.), or Building (B.)	NAME and Surname of each Person	RELATION to Head of Family	CON-DITION as to Marriage	AGE last Birthday of Males	AGE last Birthday of Females	Rank, Profession, or OCCUPATION
	E. Bourne Union			Elizabeth Harvey	Inmate	Mar		22	Cook Dom
				Ellen Warner	Do			5	Scholar
				Edith Field	Do			5	Do
				Frances Still	Do			6	Do
				William Partridge	Do		5		Do
				Caroline Luckens	Do	Wid		61	Housemaid
				Mary Vine	Do	Do		60	Dressmaker
				Emma Finch	Do	Mar		33	Do
				Jane Avery	Do	Mar		65	
				Susan Calber	Do	Do		34	General Servant
				Elizabeth Message	Do	Do		19	Kitchenmaid
				Fanny Bartholomew	Do	Do		33	
				Sarah Reed	Do	Do		41	
				Sarah Still	Do	Mar		44	Laundress
				Elizabeth Perry	Do	Do		42	Do
				Alice Weller	Do	Mar		36	Do
				Rose Williams	Do	Do		25	Dressmaker
				Foster Do	Do		1		
				Anthony A Do	Do		7wks		
				Eliza Calver	Do			1	
				Ellen Still	Do			3	
				Sarah Gordon	Do	Unm		34	Cook Dom
				Gertrude Do	Do			2	
				Frank Message	Do		7wks		
				Mary A Do	Do			7Mo	
	Total of Houses...			Total of Males and Females...			4	21	

NOTE.—Draw the pen through such of the words of the headings as are inappropriate.

LEARN TO SEARCH EFFECTIVELY

Searching the censuses can be confusing, so pick one ancestor to begin with, preferably one you already have a few details for. Hopefully, your chosen ancestor will appear in every census taken during his lifetime, and each of those censuses will give you a snapshot of his life at that time, helping you to piece together details of his life. It will also give you information about the people around him.

The unreliability of the census returns can make searching difficult, however, especially if a particular ancestor has used different names or spellings from one census return to the next. For example, he/she might have used a shortened form of a name in one census, and the full version in the next.

So your relative might appear as Alf Smith in one census, and Alfred John Smith in another.

Here are some common problems, and, where possible, how to solve them.

Missing ancestors

▶ It is estimated that around 5 per cent of people don't appear in the censuses. This could be because they were travelling on the night of the census and were therefore missed by the enumerators, or they might have been in a hospital, workhouse or prison (all of which were sometimes included but not always) or sleeping rough (common in Victorian times).

▶ Some ancestors may have deliberately gone missing – perhaps because of illegal activity.

▶ Many people, especially when the census was first introduced, objected to giving information on the grounds that it infringed their civil liberties. So many simply refused to take part in the census, despite the threat of penalties for not doing so.

▶ Some parts of the 1861 census are missing, but unless your ancestor died in infancy shortly before or after 1861, it should be possible to find him or her in either the 1851 or 1871 censuses.

TRY THIS

When you find a family in a census check the adjacent pages, as it was common for relatives to live close to each other, often in the same street.

▶ The Census Explained

Inaccuracies

▶ Ages are seldom accurate – not only were they rounded down in the 1841 census, but in this and later censuses people lied about their ages, especially women. So the census is not a reliable source of birth dates. For this information, you will need to consult official birth certificates (see pages 48–72).

▶ Birthplaces can be inaccurate. A common error was for people to state where they were brought up, which wouldn't necessarily have been their place of birth. Or sometimes they just couldn't remember and guessed. Again, birth certificates should give you more accurate information.

▶ Similarly, immigrants often said they were born in this country, fearing they would be sent back to their country of origin.

▶ Many people in Victorian times were illiterate, so either wrote things down incorrectly, or had to give the information to enumerators, who may have misspelled words or simply misheard.

▶ Problems with interpreting handwriting means that spelling errors also occurred when enumerators copied information from the census returns, and also when enumerators' books were being transcribed for online indexes. The best way around this problem is to try as many variants as you can think of when searching the indexes.

▶ People sometimes misunderstood some of the questions, and so gave incorrect information.

▶ People often lied about their occupations, either to make themselves sound more important or because they were involved in illegal activity. Prostitution among women was common in Victorian England, so women would lie on the census forms rather than admit their true occupation.

Most of the problems you are likely to encounter can be overcome by verifying the information against other sources, such as the Birth, Marriage and Death (BMD) indexes (see pages 48–72).

The 1841 census

The earliest official census is the least detailed, and therefore least likely to be of use to the family historian. But if your ancestor died before the 1851 census, you might still glean some useful information from the 1841 census – at least enough, hopefully, to give you some pointers for further research.

▶ Relationships to the main householder were not included in the 1841 census, so don't make assumptions about people sharing a surname. Victorian households often consisted of extended families, so a male adult and male child won't necessarily be father and son.

the census explained

City or Borough of

Parish or Township of *Chorley*

Enumeration Schedule.

PLACE	HOUSES		NAMES of each Person who abode therein the preceding Night.	AGE and SEX		PROFESSION, TRADE, EMPLOYMENT, or of INDEPENDENT MEANS.	Where Born	
	Uninhabited or Building	Inhabited		Males	Females		Whether Born in same County	Whether Born in Scotland, Ireland, or Foreign Parts.
Halewell			Ann Asmough		45		yes	
			Mary Do		15	Weaver	y	
			Ellen Do		9		y	
			Margaret Do		7		y	
			Betty Do		2		y	
			Ann Do		10 months		y	
do.		1	John Addison	50		Weaver	yes	
			Nanny Do		30	Do	y	
			Paul Do	20		Do	y	
			James Do	15		Piecer	y	
do.		1	William Heaton	30		Collier	yes	
			Margaret Do		35	Do	y	
			Edward Do	5			y	
			Mathew Blakely	20		Piecer	y	
			Mary Do		20	Weaver	y	
do.		1	James Winstanley	50		Weaver	yes	
			Alice Do		50		y	
			Edward Do	20		Labourer	y	
			Susan Do		15		y	
			David Hall	30		Labourer	y	
do.		1	William Blackben	40		Tailor	yes	
			Jane Do		40		y	
			Ellen Do		15		y	
			Peter Do	16		Tailor	y	
			John Do	13			y	
TOTAL in Page 12		4		11	13			

The 1911 census

Records of the 1911 census are the most detailed to date and, for the first time, the original householder pages are included as well as the enumerators' books. Information includes the kind of property your ancestor was living in (for example, a house or flat), the route taken by the enumerator and local population statistics.

CENSUS OF EN

Before writing on this Schedule please read the Examples and the Instructions given on

The contents of the Schedule will be treated as confidential. Strict care will be taken that no information is disclosed with than the

NAME AND SURNAME	RELATIONSHIP to Head of Family.	AGE (last Birthday) and SEX.		PARTICULARS as to MARRIAGE.				
of every Person, whether Member of Family, Visitor, Boarder, or Servant, who (1) passed the night of Sunday, April 2nd, 1911, in this dwelling and was alive at midnight, or (2) arrived in this dwelling on the morning of Monday, April 3rd, not having been enumerated elsewhere. No one else must be included. (For order of entering names see Examples on back of Schedule.)	State whether "Head," or "Wife," "Son," "Daughter," or other Relative, "Visitor," "Boarder," or "Servant."	For Infants under one year state the age in months as "under one month," "one month," etc.		Write "Single," "Married," "Widower," or "Widow," opposite the names of all persons aged 15 years and upwards.	State, for each Married Woman entered on this Schedule, the number of :—			
					Completed years the present Marriage has lasted. If less than one year write "under one."	Children born alive to present Marriage. (If no children born alive write "None" in Column 7).		
						Total Children Born Alive.	Children still Living.	Children who have Died.
		Ages of Males.	Ages of Females.					
1.	2.	3.	4.	5.	6.	7.	8.	9.
1 *James Douglas*	*Head*	*41*		*married*	*13*	*3*	*3*	
2 *Margaret Ann Douglas*	*wife*		*34*	*married*				
3 *Norman Douglas*	*son*	*11*						
4 *Elizabeth Irwin Douglas*	*daughter*		*6*					
5 *Isabella Douglas*	*daughter*		*1*					
6 *Elizabeth Irwin*	*Mother in law*		*73*	*widow*				
7								
8								
9								
10								
11								
12								
13								
14								
15								

(To be filled up by the Enumerator.)

I certify that :—
(1.) All the ages on this Schedule are entered in the proper sex columns.
(2.) I have counted the males and females in Columns 3 and 4 separately, and have compared their sum with the total number of persons.
(3.) After making the necessary enquiries I have completed all entries on the Schedule which appeared to be defective, and have corrected such as appeared to be erroneous.

Initials of Enumerator

	Total.		
	Males.	Females.	Persons.
	2	4	6

- The online transcriptions are probably some of the most accurate, but some errors are inevitable. Transcribing the householder pages, for example, involved deciphering the handwriting of some eight million people and, in some cases, the handwriting was illegible or contestable.
- In addition, around 5 per cent of the documents suffered water damage before they were transferred to The National Archives. Nevertheless, this is the most detailed and complete census to date, and a treasure trove for family historians.

ND AND WALES, 1911.

Number of Schedule __36__
(To be filled up by the Enumerator after collection.)

le of the paper, as well as the headings of the Columns. The entries should be written in Ink.

individual persons. The returns are not to be used for proof of age, as in connection with Old Age Pensions, or for any other purpose of Statistical Tables.

PROFESSION or OCCUPATION of Persons aged ten years and upwards.		Whether Employer, Worker, or Working on Own Account.	Whether Working at Home.	BIRTHPLACE of every person.	NATIONALITY of every Person born in a Foreign Country.	INFIRMITY.
Occupation.	Industry or Service with which this worker is connected.					
10.	11.	12.	13.	14.	15.	16.
Huryman Dresser	59 ? 59	Worker	4	Hallowell Ersdon, Gerforth	British	
	390			Gerforth		
				Gorforth		
				Gorforth		
				Gutshead 22		

(To be filled up by, or on behalf of, the Head of Family or other person in occupation, or in charge, of this dwelling.)

below the Number of Rooms in this (House, Tenement, or Apartment). the kitchen as a room but do not count landing, lobby, closet, bathroom; rehouse, office, shop.

3 rooms

I declare that this Schedule is correctly filled up to the best of my knowledge and belief.

Signature *James Douglas*

Postal Address *15 Linton ride new Gorforth*

The Census Explained

HOW TO READ A CENSUS DOCUMENT

Census documents from most years look very similar, with the exception of 1841 and 1911, so this page from the 1901 census is fairly typical of most censuses, and shows you the kind of thing you can expect to see when you download a census page.

ROAD OR STREET NAME, AND NUMBER OR NAME OF HOUSE
The address of each household was entered here – in this case the house name only (addresses in villages were often omitted), but usually included a street number and name.

This mark indicates the start of a new household.

RELATION TO HEAD OF FAMILY
This information can help to confirm family relationships.

CONDITION AS TO MARRIAGE
The marital status for each occupant is also useful for finding out more about members of your family.

AGE LAST BIRTHDAY
Ages of male occupants are listed in the left-hand column, and females in the right. Ages are not always accurate, so use these only as a guide.

Administrative County **Berkshire**

The undermentioned Ho

Civil Parish of **Shaw-cum-Donnington**

Ecclesiastical Parish of **St. Mary**

County Borough, Municipal Borough, or Urban District of

Ward or

Cols 1	2	3	4	5	6	7	8		10	11
No. of Schedule	ROAD, STREET, &c., and No. or NAME of HOUSE	HOUSES Inhabited	Uninhabited In Occupation.	Not in Occupation.	Building.	Number of Rooms occupied if less than five	Name and Surname of each Person	RELATION to Head of Family	Condition as to Marriage	Age last Birthday of
1	Shaw Rectory	1					J. Horatio Nelson	Head	M	76
							J. Eyre Nelson	Son	M	42
							Kathryn C. Nelson	Dr-in-law	M	
							Archie Keep	Servant	S	
							Alice Gibbons	Do Serv	S	
							Nellie Bates	Do Serv	S	
2	Shaw House	1					W.P. Blackburn Maze	Head	M	36
							Doris E. Blackburn Maze			
							Edith M. Blackburn Maze	Wife	M	
							Doris E. Blackburn Maze	Daur		
							Marjorie J. Blackburn Maze	Do		
							Emily A. Wilkinson	Sister	Wid	
							Richard Luffman	Servant	S	25
							Albert Giggles	Do Serv	S	22
							Barbara Landrey	Do Serv	S	
							Annie South	Do Serv	S	
							Florence Smith	Do Serv	S	
							Bessie Bevan	Do Serv	S	
							Minnie Wood	Do Serv	S	
							Rose North	Do Serv	S	
							Harriet Bush	Do Serv	S	
							Sarah Jane Cooks	Do Serv	S	
3	Home Farm	1					William Edge	Head	M	40
							Sarah A. Edge	Wife	M	
							John H. Edge	Son	S	13
							William J. Edge	Son	S	12
							Percy Edge	Son	S	9
4	Shaw Stables	1					William Moore	Head	M	44
							Irene G. Moore	Wife	M	
4	Total of Schedules of Houses and of Tenements with less than Five Rooms	4							Total of Males and of Females...		10

NOTE—Draw your pen through such words of the headings as are inapplicable.

NAME AND SURNAME OF EACH PERSON
This lists every occupant of the house on census night, with the head of the household (usually the most senior male) listed first, followed by the other occupants. Enumerators didn't always get names right, so you might need to try likely variations when searching.

PROFESSION OR OCCUPATION
This can be useful information, but bear in mind that some people exaggerated or lied about their occupations. A child was often listed as 'scholar'.

EMPLOYMENT STATUS
This tells you if someone was a worker, employed or self-employed.

WHERE BORN
The entries in this example are quite informative, but people were often vague about their birthplace so this information is not always accurate.

DISABILITIES
This indicated whether any householders were deaf and dumb, blind, imbecile, lunatic or idiot.

Marks like this were often made when the returns were being analysed.

The Census Explained

HOW MUCH DOES IT COST?

Viewing census indexes is free, but you will need to pay to see original documents or transcriptions. The costs vary, but most websites offer free trials so you can get a feel for which one best suits your needs.

Ancestry.co.uk

At the time of going to print, this website offers a free 14-day trial, after which you can choose one of four levels of membership:

Essentials membership is £10.95 a month, and gives you access to UK census records as well as the BMD indexes and other useful records.

Premium membership is £12.95 a month, and gives you additional access to parish, military, probate, immigration and Irish records.

Worldwide membership is £18.95 a month, and offers unlimited access to worldwide records as well as guaranteeing access to new releases.

Pay as you go gives you access to any 12 records over 14 days for £6.95, or 10 records over 14 days with a pre-paid voucher.

Findmypast.co.uk

Findmypast runs a similar system to Ancestry. After a 14-day trial, you can take out one of the following subscriptions:

1911 Census Only is £39.95 for six months, or £59.95 for 12 months.

Foundation gives you access to all censuses from 1841 to 1911, plus birth, marriage and death records, for £58.95 for six months or £91.95 for 12 months.

Full additionally gives you access to parish, migration, military and other specialist records for £82.95 for six months or £129.95 for 12 months.

Pay as you go starts at £6.95 for 60 credits over 90 days, and goes up to £24.95 for 280 credits over 365 days. This gives you access to all records. For census records, you will need 5 credits for a transcript from the censuses from 1841 to 1871, 1891 or 1901, and a further 5 credits for images. Transcripts for the 1881 census are free, but you will need 5 credits for an image. Costs for the 1911 census are considerably higher – 10 credits for a transcript, and 30 credits for an image.

Scotlands People (www.scotlandspeople.gov.uk)

To use this website, there is a charge of £7 to search census indexes, which gives you 30 credits over 365 days. Viewing images costs 5 credits per image, apart from the 1881 census, which costs only 1 credit. You can pay by credit or debit card, or purchase vouchers.

The Irish National Archives (www.nationalarchives.ie)

This website gives free access to census indexes and transcriptions.

BIRTH, MARRIAGE AND DEATH

By reading and following all the steps
in this chapter, you will find out:

- ▷ **How to search for your ancestors in
  the official birth, marriage and death
  indexes**

- ▷ **How to obtain certificates and what
  they will tell you**

- ▷ **How to find out more through wills
  and obituaries**

Birth, Marriage and Death

BIRTH, MARRIAGE AND DEATH CERTIFICATES: BACKGROUND

Official registration of all births, marriages and deaths began in England and Wales on 1 July 1837, although it wasn't compulsory until 1875. Inevitably inaccuracies do occur, but on the whole birth, marriage and death certificates are among the most reliable primary resources for the family historian. So once you've obtained as much information as you can from the censuses – and hopefully added some more names to your family tree – consulting the birth, marriage and death (BMD) indexes is the logical next step.

Registration districts

The country was divided into registration districts based on the groups of parishes established as Poor Law Unions in 1834 (see page 100), and each district had a superintendent registrar at its head. These districts were then further divided into sub-districts, each run by a registrar.

Each quarter, registrars would send copies of birth, marriage and death certificates to the superintendent registrar for their district, and he in turn would make quarterly returns to the General Register Office (GRO). This became the basis for the Birth, Marriage and Death (BMD) indexes.

Reorganisation of county boundaries, most notably in 1974 and 1996, has meant that many of the original registration districts have been absorbed into other districts or disappeared altogether. So you need to bear in mind that your ancestor might not necessarily be registered in the district in which you would expect to find him or her, and you might have to search in neighbouring districts.

The BMD indexes

To track down copies of your ancestors' BMD certificates, you first need to search the BMD indexes. There are two sets of indexes:

▶ The original indexes held by local register offices and compiled from the original certificates.
▶ The secondary index compiled by the General Register Office from 1837 onwards. The General Register Office indexes were compiled quarterly until 1984, when they became annual. The indexes group all births together, then marriages, then deaths.

The National Archives (see pages 108–14) holds a set of the General Register Office BMD indexes on microfilm, while your local record office will have

primary indexes available for your area and probably a copy of the General Register Office indexes as well, on microfilm or paper. Your local library might also hold or have access to copies.

Alternatively, there are a number of websites you can try if you prefer to search online (see overleaf). The big advantage with searching online is that you don't need to know the registration district (although, as with all records, the more details you have to hand the more likely you are to track down the record you are looking for).

Birth, Marriage and Death

SEARCH FOR BMD RECORDS ONLINE

As with census searches, you have to pay to view BMD entries, but one website that allows you to view records free is www.freebmd.org.uk. This is a volunteer-run site, and the transcribing of birth, marriage and death certificates is an ongoing project. It currently covers indexes from 1837 to the 1980s. Another useful website is www.ukbmd.org.uk, which charges for viewing but does give useful links to local and national indexes.

Search for a record on FreeBMD

Next step

For more information about mailing lists, see pages 192–5.

❶ Go to **www.freebmd.org.uk** and read the information page FAQs before you start, as there are lots of useful hints and tips here, including:

▶ Advice on searching the database.
▶ How to amend entries if you spot inaccuracies.
▶ How to order certificates and what they will tell you.
▶ Information about registration districts.
▶ Statistics relating to the usage of the site.
▶ How to become involved in the transcription project yourself.
▶ How to subscribe to the site's mailing lists.

- FAQ Answers to questions
  About us. Introductions

Information

● Welcome to the FreeBMD Information page.

● The website is constantly under development. We appreciate your feedback but please note that your feeeedback will be posted to the FreeBMD Administration mailing list which will be seen by all subscribers on the list. Further details about the FreeBMD mailing lists can be viewed here.

● FreeBMD is kindly hosted by The Bunker and sponsored by RootsWeb.

Reporting Problems

● If you have a correction to an entry click on the (info) button next to the entry and follow the instructions for submitting a correction.

If you experience errors while using this web site, or while submitting entries to the database, please report them to us at support@freebmd.org.uk, including

- what you were doing (i.e. submitting, searching),
- a description of the problem,
- the text of any messages,
- the link that you clicked on (the URL),
- the exact date, time and timezone when the problem occurred,
- what operating system and browser (including versions) you are using.

Thank you.

Please note that this address must **not** be used to report errors in the data held by FreeBMD; use the correction process described in the first paragraph.

General Information

- FAQ Answers to questions you might have about the project.
- About us. Introductions to the Project Team.
- FreeBMD News *(last updated 19 September 2008)*.
- Civil Registration pages. Explanations and links to other useful pages.
- Bouquets. See what people are saying about us.
- Mailing Lists. If you would like to become involved in the project, please join one of our mailing list.

2 Return to the home page, and select **Search**

3 On the next screen, make your selection from the 'Type' box on the left, then enter as many known details in the other boxes as you can. Don't worry if you only know a name and perhaps an approximation of the date; this is a start. But the more facts you know, the more refined your search will be. It is particularly good to select the correct district or county if you can, as that will narrow down your search considerably. Note that you cannot select a district and county, it has to be one or the other

4 Suppose you want to search for the birth record for an Albert Frank Browning, who you know was born somewhere in Somerset. Select **Birth** in the 'Type' box, enter his surname and first name in the appropriate boxes, select **Somerset** from the 'Counties' section and leave the 'Districts' section set at 'All Districts'. Click **Find**

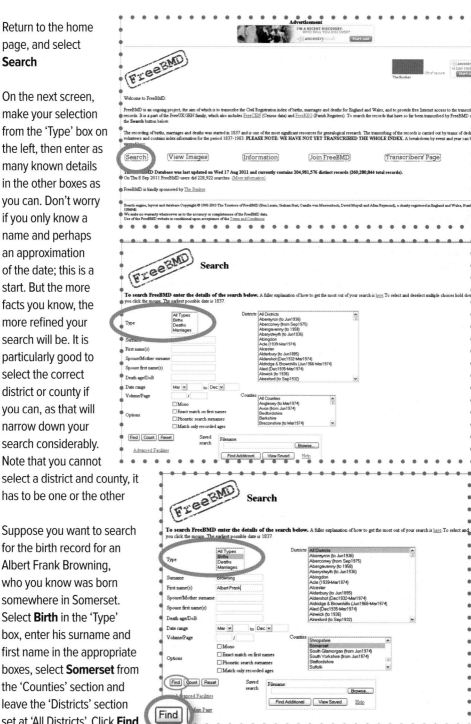

51

5 As you can see from the screenshot, this search has yielded one result – for an Albert Frank Browning, born in Bath in September 1858. If you think this might be your ancestor, click **Info**

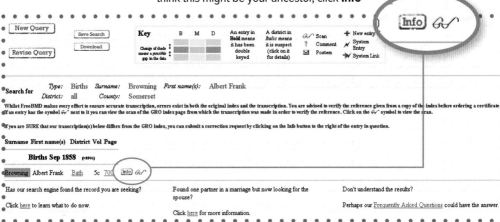

6 The next screen gives you the option to view a scan of the original document from which this information was taken and opportunities to make a correction or add a postem (additional information about the entry)

TIP

Gather as much information about an ancestor as you can before you start searching the indexes. The more search criteria you have, the more likely you are to find the record that you are looking for.

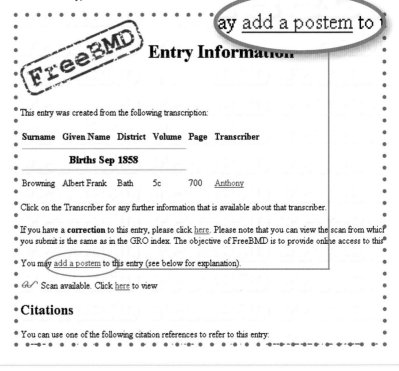

This entry was created from the following transcription:

Surname	Given Name	District	Volume	Page	Transcriber
	Births Sep 1858				
Browning	Albert Frank	Bath	5c	700	Anthony

Click on the Transcriber for any further information that is available about that transcriber.

If you have a **correction** to this entry, please click here. Please note that you can view the scan from which you submit is the same as in the GRO index. The objective of FreeBMD is to provide online access to this

You may add a postem to this entry (see below for explanation).

Scan available. Click here to view

Citations

You can use one of the following citation references to refer to this entry:

View the original document

1 To view the original document, click the glasses symbol next to 'Scan available' and click where indicated. On the next screen, choose which format you would like to view the document in (FreeBMD gives you advice on this if you are not sure; click **Help with this facility**), and then click **View the original**. A dialog box comes up, giving you the option to view or save the document. Click the option required

2 The main purpose of viewing the original document is to check the accuracy of the transcription. If you spot any errors, you can make a correction to the entry (again, FreeBMD guides you through this process: click **Help with this facility**)

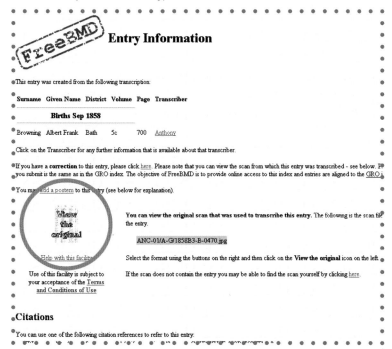

FreeBMD **Entry Information**

This entry was created from the following transcription:

Surname	Given Name	District	Volume	Page	Transcriber
Births Sep 1858					
Browning	Albert Frank	Bath	5c	700	Anthony

Click on the Transcriber for any further information that is available about that transcriber.

If you have a **correction** to this entry, please click here. Please note that you can view the scan from which this entry was transcribed - see below. If you submit is the same as in the GRO index. The objective of FreeBMD is to provide online access to this index and entries are aligned to the GRO i

You may add a postem to this entry (see below for explanation).

View the original

You can view the original scan that was used to transcribe this entry. The following is the scan file the entry.

ANC-01/A-G/1858B3-B-0470.jpg

Help with this facility

Select the format using the buttons on the right and then click on the **View the original** icon on the left.

Use of this facility is subject to your acceptance of the Terms and Conditions of Use

If the scan does not contain the entry you may be able to find the scan yourself by clicking here.

Citations

You can use one of the following citation references to refer to this entry:

3 Once you are satisfied that this is your ancestor, order the appropriate certificate from the General Register Office or the appropriate local register office (see pages 56–8 for how to order certificates)

Next step

If you've drawn a blank with the BMD indexes, you might find you can trace an ancestor through his/her occupation, religion or a variety of other sources – see pages 118–42 for other avenues to explore.

4 Once you have the certificate, you will have sufficient information to trace the line back further (see pages 59–61 for the details you can expect to find on the various certificates)

| New Query | | Save Search | | Key | B | M | D | An e⌐ |
| Revise Query | | Download | | | | | | **Bold** |

Change of shade ↕
means a possible ↕
gap in the data

Search for
Type: Deaths Surname: Browning First name(s): Albert Fra⌐
District: all County: Somerset

Whilst FreeBMD makes every effort to ensure accurate transcription, errors exist in both the original index a
If an entry has the symbol ↩ next to it you can view the scan of the GRO index page from which the transcrip⌐

If you are SURE that our transcription(s) below differs from the GRO index, you can submit a correction reque⌐

Surname First name(s) Age District Vol Page

Deaths Dec 1858 (>99%)

Browning Albert Frank Bath 5c 521 [Info] ↩

5 You can also search for more information about the same ancestor in the BMD indexes, following the same procedure to search by death and by marriage. In this case, poor Albert Frank Browning appears to have died at three months of age, a fact reinforced by a search for him in the marriage records that yields no matches. Based on this information, you can now order a death certificate for Albert Frank Browning as well

Tips when searching the indexes

▶ As with census returns, bear in mind that names might not be spelt correctly, so if you don't get a result straightaway, try different spellings – for example, Smith/Smythe.
▶ A registrar might have misheard someone's name, so try variants that sound like the name you are searching for, such as Oakes/Nokes.
▶ Allow for the possibility of transcribers misreading someone's handwriting, so an 'M' could have been mistaken for a 'W', for example.
▶ When searching the quarterly indexes, bear in mind that the date recorded is the date of registration, not the date of birth, marriage or death. Although marriage and death registration normally took place soon after the event, a birth could be registered as much as six weeks later, so that might affect which quarterly index you search in.
▶ If your ancestor was born in hospital, they might have been registered in a different district to their place of residence.

► If you can't find an entry, it could be that the event wasn't registered. Despite registration becoming compulsory in 1875, some people still slipped through the net. But it might be possible to trace a person through other members of the family, or by searching other types of records.

WHAT THE INDEXES TELL YOU

The indexes should hopefully tell you enough for you to be sure that you have tracked down the right ancestor. If you are uncertain, it's best to check the details before going to the expense of ordering a certificate – perhaps by cross-referencing to another ancestor, for example.

When searching the marriage indexes, choose the more unusual of the two surnames. You can can cross-reference this to the other person, checking that the other details match up. From 1912, the indexes include the surname of the spouse, making positive search results much more likely.

The information contained in the indexes includes:

Birth indexes
Surname
First name and middle initial
Mother's maiden name (1911 onwards)
Registration district
General Register Office references (volume number and page number)

Marriage indexes
Surname
First names
Surname of spouse (1912 onwards)
Registration district
General Register Office reference numbers

Death indexes
Surname
First names
Age (from 1866 onwards)
Registration district
General Register Office reference numbers

ORDERING CERTIFICATES

Once you have tracked down an ancestor's record in the indexes, and you are sure it is the right person, you should note down the following information, which you will need when you order copies of certificates from the General Register Office:

- ▶ Name of your ancestor.
- ▶ Year of registration.
- ▶ Volume Number.
- ▶ Page Number.

The cost is £9.25 per certificate. You can order certificates online by visiting www.gro.gov.uk/gro/content/certificates/default.asp. You will need to register first, which you can do free of charge. Alternatively, you can order over the phone on 0845 603 7788 or by post, but you will need to request an application form by emailing certificate.services@ips.gsi.gov.uk.

Find the relevant register office

Certificates are also available from the relevant local register office. You don't need the General Register Office reference to do this, but will need to find out which register office to contact. The GRO website can help here.

 Go to **www.gro.gov.uk** and click **Visit Directgov**

Home Office
**Identity &
Passport Service**

General Register Office
Official information on births, marriages and deaths

General Register Office

The General Register Office website has moved. You can now find the information you need on the following websites:

Order certificates online from the General Register Office, including birth, marriage, civil partnership, death, adoption and commemorative certificates.

 Visit Directgov for information on birth, marriage, civil partnership, death, adoption and stillbirth records and registrations, as well as guidance on researching your family history and the General Register Office indexes.

Visit the IPS website for our corporate information and announcements.

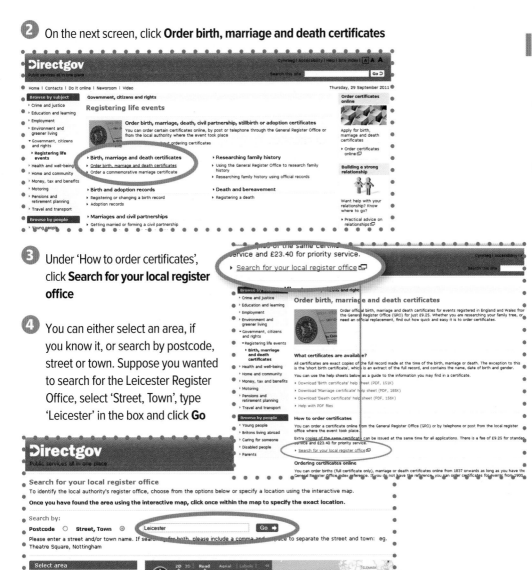

2 On the next screen, click **Order birth, marriage and death certificates**

3 Under 'How to order certificates', click **Search for your local register office**

4 You can either select an area, if you know it, or search by postcode, street or town. Suppose you wanted to search for the Leicester Register Office, select 'Street, Town', type 'Leicester' in the box and click **Go**

5 A list of areas and a map appears on your screen. Click on Leicester on the map

Directgov
Public services all in one place

● **Search for your local register office**
● To identify the local authority's register office, choose from the options below or specify a location using the interactive map.
● **Once you have found the area using the interactive map, click once within the map to specify the exact location.**

Search by:
Postcode ○   **Street, Town** ⊙   [   ] **Go ➡**
● Please enter a street and/or town name. If searching for both, please include a comma and a space to separate the street and town
● Theatre Square, Nottingham

Select area
- Leicester
- Oadby and Wigston
- Blaby
- Harborough
- North West Leicestershire
- Charnwood
- Melton Mowbray
- Hinckley and Bosworth
- Rutland
- Nuneaton and Bedworth
- Rushcliffe
- Rutland

6 The contact details for Leicester Register Office will come up on your screen. An 'X' on the map pinpoints the location of the Register Office; hover your mouse over this, and a box comes up giving you the option of more details and directions

Leicester City Council – Register Office

Town Hall
Town Hall Square
Leicester Road
LE1 9BG

More Details...
Get Directions...

7 Click **More details** and then **Visit Site** to go to the Leicester Register Office website

Leicester City Council   [search] A-Z I How Do I?

Advice & Benefits | Business | Community & Living | Council & Democracy | Education & Learning | Environment & Planning | Health & Social Care | Housing | Jobs & Careers | Leisure Culture | Transport & Streets

Council & Democracy

Home > Your Council & Services > Council & Democracy > Births, Marriages and Deaths

Council & Democracy
Births, Marriages and Deaths
- Births
- Contact Us
- Copy Certificates
- Deaths
- Coroners
- Marriages
- Still-births
- Civil Partnerships
- Table of Statutory Registration Service Fees
- Renewal of Vows
- Naming Ceremonies
- Nationality Checking Service
- Travel & Parking Information
- Our Service to You

Births, Marriages and Deaths

If you wish to register a birth or death, give notice of marriage or civil partnership or use the nationality checking service in Leicester, you will need to book an appointment at Leicester Register Office.

WHAT THE CERTIFICATES TELL YOU

You can glean a lot of useful information from the civil registration certificates, which should help fill in some gaps in your family tree.

Birth certificates

▶ Date and place of birth.
▶ Time of birth if it is a multiple birth (in which case you will need to do further searches to find a possible twin, triplet, etc.).
▶ Place of birth.
▶ Child's name and gender.
▶ Father's name (if this column is blank, the child is probably illegitimate).
▶ Mother's name, surname and maiden name.
▶ Father's occupation.
▶ Place of residence of the informant (usually the mother).
▶ Signature.
▶ Date of registration.

CERTIFIED COPY OF AN ENTRY OF BIRTH
COPI DILYS O GOFNOD GENEDIGAETH

GIVEN AT THE **GENERAL REGISTER OFFICE**
FE'I RHODDWYD YN Y **GENERAL REGISTER OFFICE**

Application Number } **PAS 2050065**
Rhif y Cais

REGISTRATION DISTRICT } **Llanfyllin**
DOSBARTH COFRESTRU

1841 BIRTH in the Sub-district of } **Llanfair** in the **County of Montgomery**
GENEDIGAETH yn Is-ddosbarth yn

Columns- Colofnau No. Rhif	1 When and where born Pryd a lle y ganwyd	2 Name, if any Enw os oes un	3 Sex Rhyw	4 Name and surname of father Enw a chyfenw'r tad	5 Name, surname and maiden surname of mother Enw, cyfenw a chyfenw morwynol y fam	6 Occupation of father Gwaith y tad	7 Signature, description and residence of informant Llofnod, disgrifiad a chyfeiriad yr hysbysydd	8 When registered Pryd y cofrestrwyd	9 Signature of registrar Llofnod y cofrestrydd	10 Name entered after registration Enw a gofnodwyd wedi'r cofrestru
40	Twenty birth December 1840 at Llwyfanwy Llanggynu	Margarett	Girl	David Jones	Margarett Jones formerly Jones	Labourer	The mark of X David Jones Father Llwyfanwy Llanggynu	Second of February 1841	Griffith Jones Registrar	

CERTIFIED to be a true copy of an entry in the certified copy of a Register of Births in the District above mentioned.
TYSTIOLAETHWYD ei fod yn gopi cywir o gofnod mewn copi y tystiwyd iddo o Gofrestr Genedigaethau yn y Dosbarth a enwyd uchod.

Given at the GENERAL REGISTER OFFICE, under the Seal of the said Office
Fe'i rhoddwyd yn y GENERAL REGISTER OFFICE, o dan Sêl y Swyddfa a enwyd.

the **9th** day of **September** } **2005**
y dydd o fis

CAUTION: THERE ARE OFFENCES RELATING TO FALSIFYING OR ALTERING A CERTIFICATE AND USING OR POSSESSING
A FALSE CERTIFICATE. © CROWN COPYRIGHT

GOFAL: MAE YNA DROSEDDAU YN YMWNEUD Â FFUGIO NEU ADDASU TYSTYSGRIF NEU
DOEFNYDDIO TYSTYSGRIF FFUG NEU WRTH FOD AG UN YN EICH MEDDIANT. © HAWLFRAINT Y GORON

WBXZ 182413

WARNING: A CERTIFICATE IS NOT EVIDENCE OF IDENTITY.
RHYBUDD: NID YW TYSTYSGRIF YN PROFI PWY YDYCH CHI.

Marriage certificates

▶ Parish in which the marriage took place (traditionally the bride's home parish).
▶ Date of marriage.
▶ Full names of bride and groom.
▶ Ages of bride and groom (often inaccurate!).
▶ Marital status (bachelor, spinster, widow, widower).
▶ Occupations (often for the groom only).
▶ Places of residence at time of marriage.
▶ Names and occupations of fathers.
▶ Whether the marriage was by banns or licence.
▶ Signatures of bride, groom and two witnesses.
▶ Name of the clergyman officiating at the ceremony.

CERTIFIED COPY OF AN ENTRY OF MARRIAGE   GIVEN AT THE GENERAL REGISTER OFFICE

Application Number   PAS1040964

1864. Marriage solemnized at *the Parish Church* in the *Parish of Hackney* in the County of *Middlesex*

No.	When Married.	Name and Surname.	Age.	Condition.	Rank or Profession.	Residence at the time of Marriage.	Father's Name and Surname.	Rank or Profession of Father.
445	June 25th 1864	Edwin James Pilton	full age	Bachelor	Labourer	Morning Lane	James Pilton	Labourer
		Margaret Jones	full age	Spinster	—	Morning Lane	Edward Jones	Labourer

Married in the *Parish Church* according to the Rites and Ceremonies of the Established Church, by _____ or after *Banns* by me, *Alexr Gordon*

This Marriage was solemnized between us, { *Edwin James Pilton* } in the Presence of us, { *Richard Ward* }
{ *Margaret Jones x her mark* } { *Sophia Coburn* }

CERTIFIED to be a true copy of an entry in the certified copy of a register of Marriages in the Registration District of   **Hackney**

Given at the GENERAL REGISTER OFFICE, under the Seal of the said Office, the   **9th**   day of   **February   2005**

MXB 927585

This certificate is issued in pursuance of section 65 of the Marriage Act 1949. Sub-section 3 of that section provides that any certified copy of an entry purporting to be sealed or stamped with the seal of the General Register Office shall be received as evidence of the marriage to which it relates without any further or other proof of the entry, and no certified copy purporting to have been given in the said Office shall be of any force or effect unless it is sealed or stamped as aforesaid.

CAUTION: THERE ARE OFFENCES RELATING TO FALSIFYING OR ALTERING A CERTIFICATE AND USING OR POSSESSING A FALSE CERTIFICATE. ©CROWN COPYRIGHT

WARNING: A CERTIFICATE IS NOT EVIDENCE OF IDENTITY.

MB

Death certificates

▶ Date and place of death.
▶ Forename and surname of the deceased.
▶ Gender.
▶ Occupation.
▶ Cause of death (in the 19th century, this was often vague).
▶ Age (from 1866 – again, often inaccurate).
▶ Date of birth (from 1869).
▶ Name, address and signature of informant (could be a relative or doctor).
▶ Date of registration.
▶ Signature of registrar.

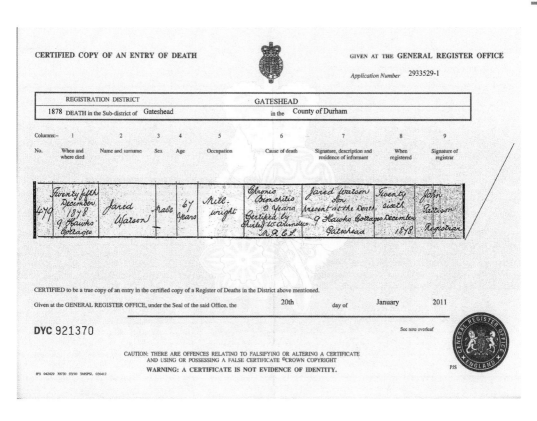

BMD RECORDS IN SCOTLAND

Registration became compulsory in Scotland on 1 January 1855, and you can search the indexes and download copies of certificates at www.scotlandspeople.gov.uk. Scotland's certificates and indexes are generally more detailed than those for England and Wales, so if you are tracing Scottish ancestry, they can cut out a lot of the detective work. In addition to the details provided in England and Wales, Scottish records include the following:

Birth

▶ Parents' ages and birthplaces, and details of other children (1855 certificates only).

▶ Date and place of parents' marriage (1855 certificates and from 1861 onwards).

▶ Time of child's birth (not just for multiple births, as in England and Wales).

▶ Mother's maiden name on birth indexes from 1929 onwards.

Page 454.

18_68_. BIRTHS in the _Central_ of District _____ in the _Burgh_ of _Glasgow_

No.	Name and Surname.	When and Where Born.	Sex.	Name, Surname, & Rank or Profession of Father. Name, and Maiden Surname of Mother. Date and Place of Marriage.	Signature and Qualification of Informant, and Residence, if out of the House in which the Birth occurred.	When and Where Registered, and Signature of Registrar.
1360	Charles Rennie McIntosh	1868 June Seventh 11 h 15 m A.M. 70 Parson Street Glasgow	M	William McIntosh Police Clerk Margaret McIntosh M.S. Rennie 1862 August 4th Glasgow	W. McIntosh Father present	1868 June 25th at Glasgow Arch. Hood Apost. Registrar. 36
1361	Rose Ann Caldwell	1868 May Thirty First 10 h 10 m A.M. 12 Forth Street Glasgow	F	William Caldwell Iron Moulder Mary Caldwell M.S. McSheffray 1866 January 8th Glasgow	Mary Caldwell Mother	1868 June 25th at Glasgow Arch. Hood Apost. Registrar. 38
1362	Walter Dalgliesh Jackson	1868 June Eighteenth 1h 0m P.M. 58 North St Anderson Glasgow	M	Walter Dalgliesh Jackson Railway Clerk Jane Jackson M.S. Dunlop 1864 June 15th Glasgow	W. B. Jackson Father Present	1868 June 26th at Glasgow Arch. Hood Apost. Registrar. 36

B

Thomas Davidson Registrar

Marriage

▶ Full name, age, occupation and usual residence of the bride and groom.
▶ Date and place of marriage.
▶ Names of the parents of the bride and groom (including mothers' maiden names), plus father's occupation.
▶ Whether the couple married in a church or by agreement ('irregular' marriages – where a man and woman were regarded as a couple by cohabitation or consummation – were legal in Scotland until 1940, and could be formalised by obtaining a warrant from a Justice of the Peace or Sheriff)
▶ Details of any previous marriages and children (up to 1855 only).
▶ Birthplaces of the bride and groom (up to 1855 only).
▶ Signature of witnesses and registrar.
▶ Where the marriage was registered.
▶ Women indexed under married and maiden names.

Death

▶ Birthplace of the deceased, and how long in place of residence at time of death (1855 only).
▶ Name of spouse and children (1855 only).
▶ Details of the place of burial and name of undertaker (1855–61).
▶ Name of parents (including mother's maiden name) on certificates (1861 onwards).
▶ Indexes include ages (from 1868), birth dates (from 1969) and mother's maiden name (from 1974).

These extra details can make it much easier to trace the family back a few more generations. For example, if you have found the death certificate for Great Uncle Jock, you can now trace his wife and parents as well, which extends your family tree outwards and upwards. Once you have found records for his wife and parents, they will reveal the names and details of further relatives, and so on.

BE CAREFUL

Although these extra details can be a godsend, bear in mind that some information, particularly relating to parents, can be inaccurate so cross-check with other sources.

birth, marriage and death

BMD RECORDS IN IRELAND

Registration began in Ireland on 1 April 1845 for Protestant marriages, and for all births, marriages and deaths on 1 January 1864. Although many Irish records were lost when the Public Record Office was destroyed by a fire in 1922, the good news is that the civil records of births, marriages and deaths are among the many that survived.

To find records relating to Ireland, a good starting point is www.familysearch. org, which contains details of births, baptisms, marriages and deaths from 1660, although it doesn't include records for Northern Ireland after the Partition of 1922. But if you're not sure whereabouts in Ireland your ancestor came from, it's worth trying here first.

1 Go to **www.familysearch.org**, scroll down to 'Browse by location' and select **Europe**

BE CAREFUL

From 1864, people could be fined if a birth was not registered within three months. This means that poor people sometimes 'fiddled' the date to avoid having to pay.

2 On the next screen, under 'Place', click **Ireland**

3 From the list of records on the next screen, click the one that you want, for example, **Ireland Births and Baptisms 1620–1881**

4 Suppose you want to search for the birth of a relative named John O'Leary, on the next screen enter the name into the relevant boxes and click **Search**

5 On the list of results, scroll through to see if any look a likely match for your relative. You can get more details by clicking on the

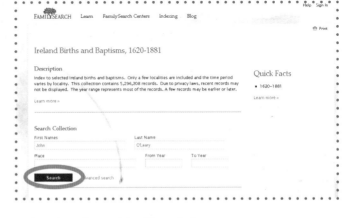

down arrow on the far right-hand side – this tells you John O'Leary's date and place of birth, and the names of his parents. This information can help to identify family relationships, confirm known or suspected details, and direct you to the source of the original record

FAMILYSEARCH   Learn   FamilySearch Centers   Indexing   Blog   Help   Sign In

Refine your search   ▼ Ireland Births and Baptisms, 1620-1881
Search all collections
1–20 of 5,206 results for >Name: **John O'Leary**

Filter your results by:
Learn more

Try adding more search terms to improve your search results.

Collections
Birth, Marriage, & Death (5,206)
  Ireland Births and Baptisms, 1620-1881 (5,206)
Birthplace
Birth Year
Residence Place
Residence Year
Gender

John O Leary   birth: 04 Mar 1867   parents:
Ireland Births and Baptisms, 1620–1881   Cork, Ireland   William O Leary, Eliza O Donnell
                    residence: 1867
                    Ireland

John O Leary   birth: 11 Jan 1867   parents:
Ireland Births and Baptisms, 1620–1881   Cork, Ireland   John O Leary, Ellen Ellis
                    residence: 1867
                    Ireland

John   birth: 04 Mar 1867   parents:
Ireland Births and Baptisms, 1620–1881   Milford, Cork, Ire   William O Leary, Eliza O Donnell
                    residence: 1867
                    , , Cork, Ireland

John   birth: 11 Jan 1867   parents:
Ireland Births and Baptisms, 1620–1881   Cork, The City Of Cork, Ire   John O Leary, Ellen Ellis
                    residence: 1867
                    , , Cork, Ireland

birth, marriage and death

Another useful online source covering the whole of Ireland is www. irelandgenweb.com, which has detailed indexes searchable by surname or county. This is a volunteer project constantly being added to.

An alternative resource for Northern Ireland (which encompasses the six counties of Antrim, Armagh, Down, Fermanagh, Londonderry and Tyrone) is the website of the Public Record Office (PRO) of Northern Ireland (www.proni. gov.uk). It gives access to the entire PRO archive of over a million items, with new records constantly being added.

Copies of birth, marriage or death certificates can be obtained from the General Register Office of Northern Ireland in Belfast (www.groni.gov.uk) or, for the Republic of Ireland, from the General Register Office in Dublin (www. groireland.ie).

BMD RECORDS IN THE CHANNEL ISLANDS

Civil registration began at different times throughout the Channel Islands, as follows:

Jersey

August 1842: births, marriages and deaths. Indexes are held on microfiche at the Jersey Archive in St Helier (www.jerseyheritage.org), in the Channel Islands Family History Society Research Room. An appointment is necessary if you want to visit in person. The website also has useful downloadable leaflets about researching family history in Jersey.

Copies of certificates can be obtained from the Judicial Greffe (www.gov.je/ Government/NonexecLegal/JudicialGreffe/Pages/index.aspx).

Guernsey, Herm, Lihou, Jethou and Brecqhou

(These islands, together with Alderney and Sark, are known as the Bailiwick of Guernsey)
October 1840: births and deaths
January 1841: non-Anglican marriages
1919: all marriages

Records are held at Her Majesty's Greffier in St Peter Port (www.gov.gg), and you can also obtain copies of certificates from here. The Priaulx Library (www. priaulxlibrary.co.uk) also has incomplete sets of records on microfilm.

Alderney

1850: births and deaths

1886: marriages

Indexes and copies of certificates are available at The Greffier at St Anne in Alderney (www.alderney.gov.gg) up to 1925; after that date records are held by Her Majesty's Greffier in Guernsey. There are some records missing, mostly from the 1850s to 1870s, but there are books of declaration available that should supply the missing details.

Sark

1915: deaths

1919: marriages

1925: births

Civil registration records from 1925 only are held by the Greffier in Sark (www.gov.sark.gg).

BMD RECORDS FOR THE ISLE OF MAN

Civil registration of births and deaths began in 1878, with marriages added in 1884. However, registration for births was available in 1821, so some civil records date back to then.

Records for the Isle of Man can be found at the Manx National Heritage Library and Archives in the capital town of Douglas, which has a large collection of records and indexes, many on microfilm or microfiche, including the BMD index from 1878 to 1993. Unlike many libraries and archives, no appointment is necessary. Indexes are also accessible online at www.gov.im/mnh/heritage/library/nationallibrary.xml. The website includes downloadable leaflets on researching Manx family history, which you might find useful.

Copies of birth, marriage and death certificates can be obtained from the General Register Office in Douglas (www.gov.im/infocentre), which has a downloadable form on the website.

WILLS AND PROBATE RECORDS

Wills can provide a wealth of information about your family. Because people generally leave property to close family, you could find details of children, nieces, nephews and siblings, all of which can either confirm information gleaned from censuses and civil registration records, or even mention family members you never knew existed.

The size of a legacy and details of property distributed can also tell you a lot about your ancestor as a person, helping to make him or her 'real' and not just a name on a piece of paper. People have often left bizarre instructions in their wills, or bequeathed money to a favourite charity, and this all helps to build up a picture of your ancestor's character, likes and dislikes, and lifestyle.

Where someone died intestate, members of their immediate family could apply for a letter of administration to authorise them to wind up the estate. Letters of administration (usually abbreviated to Admon.) are not as useful to the family historian, but can nevertheless reveal some useful details about the deceased and their immediate next of kin.

What can you find out from a will?

Useful information in wills includes:

- Names and addresses of living relatives, either in the UK or possibly other parts of the world.
- Names and other details of deceased relatives.
- Clarifying relationships between family members. For example, you might have identified a female ancestor but been unsure exactly where she fitted into the family tree – a will naming her as someone's daughter helps to put another piece in your jigsaw.
- Clarifying identities where there is more than one person with the same name.
- Clarifying the marital status of a daughter or niece, and possibly giving the names of their husbands.
- Naming relatives you didn't know existed (both living and deceased).
- Revealing some possible family skeletons, such as the existence of an illegitimate child or mistress.
- Providing insight into the wealth, lifestyle and personality of your ancestor.

Where to search for wills

From 11 January 1858, the responsibility of proving authenticity of wills and letters of administration passed from the Anglican church to the state. District probate offices were established, which sent copies to the Principal Probate

Jargon buster

Letters of administration
A Letter of Administration could be issued to surviving members of a family if their relative died intestate. In such a case, family members could apply for a Letter of Administration, entitling them to manage the estate.

BE CAREFUL

Don't assume that all the deceased's relatives are stated in the will – there could be others who, for a variety of reasons, were not included. A disgraced son, for example, might be excluded.

Registry in London. This is now part of the Probate Service, which also consists of 11 district probate registries and 18 probate sub-registries throughout England and Wales.

Annual indexes of wills and letters of administration (known as the National Probate Calendar) from 1858 to the present day can be viewed by visiting the Probate Service offices in London (see below), but it is advisable to make an appointment first. Alternatively, you can view the indexes online at websites such as www.ancestry.co.uk, which allows you to search by name and approximate year of probate.

You can also view the indexes on microfiche at The National Archives (www.nationalarchives.gov.uk), at the Institute of Heraldic and Genealogical Studies (www.ihgs.ac.uk) or at your local record office.

Information included in the indexes includes:
▶ Deceased's residence at time of death.
▶ Date of death.
▶ Details of executors and administrators.

Obtaining copies of wills

Once you have found your ancestor's will in the National Probate Calendar, you can order a copy from the Probate Service. There are a number of ways to do this:

▶ By post from the Postal Searches and Copies Department, Leeds District Probate Registry, York House, York Place, Leeds LS1 2BA. You will first need to download an order form from the website www.justice.gov.uk/guidance/courts-and-tribunals/courts/probate/family-history.htm.
▶ In person at the London Probate Department, PRFD, First Avenue House, 42–49 High Holborn, 7th Floor, Holborn, London WC1V 6NP, tel: 020 7947 6939.
▶ In person at any of the District Probate Registries or Probate Sub-registries – these are listed on the Probate Service website (www.justice.gov.uk/guidance/courts-and-tribunals/courts/probate/index.htm).

The fee for a single search within a four-year period, together with a copy of the will, is £5. If the search extends beyond four years, the fee is an extra £3 for each four-year period. So the more accurately you are able to pinpoint the likely date of probate, the cheaper it will be.

birth, marriage and death

DID YOU KNOW?
Before the 1882 Married Women's Property Act, the property of a married woman officially belonged to her husband, so up to that date it is rare to find wills written by women other than by spinsters and widows.

TRY THIS
Probate could take up to three years after death, so bear in mind that it could take a while to find the record you are looking for. If you can't find anything after three years from the date of death, try searching in the year another family member died, as that is often the time that unadministered estates are discovered.

TIP
For wills pre-1858, see pages 96–9.

Obtaining wills outside England and Wales

If your ancestor's place of residence at the time of death was outside England and Wales, you will need to contact the relevant authority, as detailed below.

Scotland

HM Commissary Office, 27 Chambers Street, Edinburgh EH1 2NS, tel: 0131 247 2850 (for deaths after 1985).
Scottish Records Office, HM General Register House, Edinburgh EH1 3YY, tel: 0131 535 1334 (for deaths before 1985).

Northern Ireland

Probate Office, The Royal Courts of Justice, Belfast BT1 3JF, tel: 028 9072 4672 (for deaths within the last seven years).
Public Record Office of Northern Ireland, 66 Balmoral Street, Belfast BT9 6NY, tel: 028 9025 1318 (for deaths occurring more than seven years ago).

Republic of Ireland

Probate Office, 15–24 Phoenix Street North, Smithfield, Dublin 7, tel: +353 (0)1 888 6174 (for records less than 20 years old).
National Archives Office, Bishop Street, Dublin 8, tel: +353 (0)1 407 2300 (for records more than 20 years old).

Isle of Man

General Registry, Deemster's Walk, Bucks Road, Douglas IM1 3AR, tel: 01624 687039.

Channel Islands

Addresses for the Channel Islands are the same as for obtaining birth, marriage and death certificates (see pages 66–7).

OBITUARIES

An obituary can be a wonderful way of discovering more about your ancestor's life, and might, in fact, be the only biographical sketch in existence. Obituaries might also give you a few more details that you can either add to your family tree or use as clues to find out more. Sometimes they can help clarify known or suspected facts. Not everybody will have obituaries, of course; generally, a person has to achieve something noteworthy – such as having an outstanding career, being a war hero or working for charity – to warrant an obituary at either national or local level. Sometimes he/she might have an obituary due to notoriety rather than fame – perhaps one of your ancestors has a criminal past!

The kind of information you might get about an ancestor from an obituary includes the following:
- ▶ Full name and, in the case of a female ancestor, a maiden name.
- ▶ Place of residence at time of death.
- ▶ Whether he/she died at home or in a hospital/nursing home/hospice.
- ▶ Cause of death.

- Age at death.
- Details of inquest if the death was sudden or suspicious.
- When and where the funeral took place.
- Names of other family members.
- Career details and achievements.
- Company he/she worked for, position(s) in that company, and how many years there.
- Other noteworthy facts, such as charity projects, for example, or being a leading light in the local operatic society.

If your ancestor was famous, there was probably an obituary in one of the national papers – indexes exist for *The Times* and the *Manchester Guardian* (now just the *Guardian*) in many local libraries, as well as the British Library Newspapers at Colindale Avenue in London (http://newspapers.bl.uk/blcs/). You will need a subscription to make full use of the research facilities on this website. For people who were noteworthy locally, you can search the archives of the relevant local newspapers, which should be available in local libraries. If your ancestor died in a different area to the one he was born in, you could try the local newspapers for both areas, as both might carry obituaries, and you might glean different facts from each. It's also worth checking local newspapers for national celebrities as they could well be given an obituary in the area in which they were born, lived or died.

Other useful websites

- There is an obituary collection for the UK and Ireland at www.ancestry.co.uk, where you can search free but will have to pay to access records (see page 46 for details of costs). Most of these are recent, but a great resource if you are looking for recently deceased relatives.
- Rootsweb has a free searchable index of English obituaries at http://archiver. rootsweb.com/th/index/ENGLISH-OBITS.
- If your ancestor played a part in politics, you might find him/her in the *Guardian*'s online obituaries at www.guardian.co.uk/politics/obituaries, although this only goes back to 1986.

BEFORE CIVIL REGISTRATION

By reading and following all the steps in this chapter, you will find out how to:

▶ **Search the parish registers for details of your ancestors' baptisms, marriages and deaths**

▶ **Discover what gravestones can tell you about your family**

▶ **Learn about your family paupers**

Before Civil Registration

GOING FURTHER BACK IN TIME

Once you have discovered as much as you can about your ancestry from the civil registers and census returns, it's time to take a step back and start delving further into the past. Records before civil registration are not always as detailed or complete as the later records, especially as the earliest record-keeping was fairly haphazard. Nevertheless, there are plenty of useful resources to help you take your family tree back a few more generations.

Parish registers

These are the most useful records for pre-1837 research, and therefore your best starting point. From 1538, Anglican church ministers had to keep weekly registers of baptisms, marriages and burials for every parish in England and Wales, on the orders of Thomas Cromwell, Henry VIII's Vicar General.

In Scotland, Old Parochial Registers date from around 1558, although in the Highlands record-keeping didn't begin until the mid-18th century.

The first registers were kept on loose sheets of paper, often of very poor quality, and many were subsequently lost or damaged, so very few records from before 1600 have survived. But changes to the way records were kept and the amount of information recorded meant that the system gradually improved, and the surviving records are a vast and essential source for the family historian. For many, the parish registers may be the only places where ancestors get a mention.

How record-keeping changed

Bishops' Transcripts (sometimes referred to as register bills) were created in 1597, when copies of parish registers were bound in volumes and sent annually to each diocesan bishop. Sometimes the Bishops' Transcripts contain details not found in the registers and, in some cases, have survived where parish registers have not.

Hardwicke's Marriage Act of 1754 required parishes to keep separate registers of marriages in pre-printed books. Until then, baptisms, marriages and deaths were usually recorded in the same handwritten registers, and the information recorded varied from one parish to another.

Rose's Act of 1812 decreed that baptisms and burials should also be kept in standardised, pre-printed registers, with a unique number allocated to each record. Before then, baptisms and burials were often listed chronologically in the same register, making it easy to confuse the two.

WHAT THE PARISH REGISTERS TELL YOU

Parish registers may not be as detailed or easy to find as civil registers, but they can still give you some useful information. The birth, marriage and death information that might be available on the registers is listed here.

Baptisms

Before 1812:

- ▶ Child's name.
- ▶ Date of baptism.
- ▶ Father's name in some cases.
- ▶ Occasionally mother's name, father's occupation and grandparents' names.

After the introduction of Rose's Act in 1812:

- ▶ Child's forenames.
- ▶ Date and place of baptism.
- ▶ Father's full name, occupation and address.
- ▶ Mother's forenames.
- ▶ In the case of an illegitimate child, full details of the mother only.

Marriages

Before 1754:

- ▶ Date of marriage.
- ▶ Full names of bride and groom.
- ▶ Sometimes other information; varies according to parish.

BE CAREFUL

Baptisms often took place months or even years after the birth, so don't be tempted to use a baptism as a reliable indicator of someone's date of birth. It may not be possible to find a birth date, so you will have to record it on your family tree as 'bpt.' for 'baptism'.

DID YOU KNOW?

Anybody could witness a marriage, so witnesses named in marriage registers were not necessarily related to the bride or groom. It's just as likely that they were close friends or even casual acquaintances.

Before Civil Registration

TRY THIS

If you can't find your ancestor in the parish registers, try searching for a close relative such as a sibling or cousin, which might help point you in the right direction.

After Hardwicke's Marriage Act of 1754:

- ▶ Date and place of marriage.
- ▶ Groom's full name, occupation and home parish.
- ▶ Bride's forenames, maiden name and home parish.
- ▶ Whether married by licence or banns (see below).
- ▶ For both bride and groom, whether spinster/bachelor/widower.
- ▶ Signatures of bride and groom (or, if illiterate, some kind of mark).
- ▶ Signatures or marks of two witnesses.

Burials

Before 1812:

- ▶ Name of deceased only in earliest registers.
- ▶ Age, occupation, marital status and place of residence of the deceased (varied from one parish to another).

After Rose's Act of 1812:

- ▶ Age at death.
- ▶ Full name of the deceased.
- ▶ Date of death.
- ▶ Address at time of death.

Marriage licences and banns

Marriage banns, in which a couple's intention to marry was called out in church, dates back to 1215, and were intended to prevent bigamy. Sometimes you will see marriage banns recorded in parish registers with details of the marriage itself, or they may have been recorded in separate banns registers, which are usually stored in record offices alongside the parish registers.

Marriage licences were introduced in the 14th century and were a quick way of tying the knot – useful if the bride was pregnant. They were issued by the ecclesiastical courts, on receipt of a bond stating a sum of money payable if the marriage was later found to be illegal. Few marriage licences survived, but those that have are usually to be found with parish registers.

LOCATE A PARISH REGISTER

If you know the parish in which your ancestor was baptised, married or buried, a good starting point is The Phillimore Atlas and Index of Parish Registers, edited by Cecil R. Humphrey-Smith (3rd edition, 2003). This comprehensive guide includes the following information:

- ▶ Full list of parishes in England, Wales and Scotland up to the mid-1830s, with details of where original registers and copies/transcripts are held.
- ▶ Whether the registers have been indexed, and if so, where the indexes can be found.
- ▶ Dates covered by surviving registers.
- ▶ Details of old registration districts.
- ▶ Maps showing old parish boundaries, together with contemporary maps showing their modern equivalents.
- ▶ Maps showing historic county boundaries.

The book currently retails at £50. Alternatively, copies might be available in your library or local studies centre.

The Genuki website, www.genuki.org.uk, also gives useful information about the location of parish registers on their county pages, along with contact details and opening hours of county record offices.

The International Genealogical Index (IGI) is an excellent resource for tracing records for baptisms and marriages (but note that burials are not included). It was compiled by the LDS from a combination of original parish registers, Bishops' Transcripts and non-parochial registers from the 16th century up to the beginning of the 20th century. Microfiche copies of the IGI are available for viewing at county record offices, local studies centres, LDS family history centres and the Society of Genealogists. Information included in each index entry includes:

- ▶ Surname.
- ▶ Forename(s).
- ▶ Event associated with the named person (either baptism or marriage).
- ▶ Date of event.
- ▶ Location of event (parish, county and country).
- ▶ Names of parents (if baptism).
- ▶ Name of spouse (if marriage).
- ▶ Batch number of original document.

BE CAREFUL

Parish registers are organised by historical county, so you need to be aware of county boundary changes. Sometimes, when a parish has moved from one county to another, the original registers are held by the historical county and copies by the new county, which is very helpful for family historians.

TRY THIS

The Genuki website is an extensive and indispensable resource for the family historian, with lots of useful information and links to other websites. It is worth bookmarking on your computer, as you might want to return to it again and again.

The British Isles Vital Records Index (BVRI) is a supplement to the IGI, and contains around 10 million baptism and 2 million marriage records in England and Wales from 1538 to 1888 that are not included in the IGI. You can view the BVRI at most record and local studies centres, the LDS family history centres and the Society of Genealogists.

Boyd's Marriage Index might prove useful if you can't find your ancestor in any of the above sources. It covers English marriages from 1538 to 1837, but its coverage is patchy, varying considerably from one county to another. Information includes:

▶ Full names of bride and groom.
▶ Year of marriage.
▶ Parish and county in which marriage took place.
▶ Source (parish registers, Bishops' Transcripts, or marriage licences and banns).

The original index is held by The Society of Genealogists, with microfiche copies and transcriptions available at some record offices and local studies centres. You can also find it online at the subscription site www.origins.net, which includes lots of useful information and search tips for the index.

National Burial Index (NBI) The NBI was compiled by the Federation of Family History Societies (www.ffhs.org.uk) to complement the IGI, and it contains over 18 million names from England and Wales, drawn from parish, non-conformist and cemetery registers. It can be obtained from the FFHS on CD, or it is available online at www.findmypast.co.uk, where you can search free but need to pay to view. Information includes:

▶ County, parish and cemetery in which burial took place.
▶ Date of burial.
▶ Surname and forename(s) of the deceased.
▶ Age at death.

BE CAREFUL

Although the indexes are invaluable for locating documents and giving basic information, always consult the original document if you can, as they contain more details, and errors do arise in transcripts and compilations.

VIEW A PARISH REGISTER

Once you know which parish register contains the information you are looking for, you can research your relatives' lives from any of the following places.

County record offices (or their equivalents – many such offices have been absorbed into local studies or history centres) are the main repositories for original parish registers. Some also have copies on microfiche/film. They also hold Bishops' Transcripts, originally held by Diocese offices.

The National Library of Wales holds copies of parish registers for over 500 parishes in Wales (www.llgc.org.uk). The website has limited search facilities, so you will need to visit the library to take full advantage of its holdings.

The National Records for Scotland (formed in April 2011 from the merger of The National Archives for Scotland and the General Register Office for Scotland) holds Old Parochial Registers, as well as Non-conformist and Catholic registers. Until the new NRS website is up and running, you can still use the two existing websites (www.nas.gov.uk and www.gro-scotland.gov.uk).

The National Archives of Ireland (www.nationalarchives.ie) and the **Public Record Office of Northern Ireland** (www.proni.gov.uk) hold transcripts of Protestant registers (few original church records survive in Ireland). The National Library of Ireland (www.nli.ie) has microfilm copies of surviving Roman Catholic registers.

The Society of Genealogists (www.sog.org.uk) holds one of the UK's largest collections of transcripts on microfiche/film, including the parish registers for England and Wales, and the Old Parochial Registers for Scotland. They have also published transcriptions of parish registers in county guides.

Family History Centres hold microfilmed copies of registers. There are about a hundred centres scattered across England, Wales, Scotland and Ireland. To find a centre near you, visit the LDS website, www.familysearch.org, click **Library** and then **Family History Centres**. Select your country from the drop-down menu and a list of centres will come up on the screen.

Family history societies often have copies of parish registers available for purchase. For details of family history societies for each area, visit the official website of the Federation of Family History Societies at www.ffhs.org.uk.

TIP
CD-Roms with scanned images of registers are available to purchase from S&N Genealogy supplies.

SEARCH ONLINE FOR PARISH REGISTER ENTRIES

To search for parish register entries online, try websites such as www.familysearch.org and http://freereg.rootsweb.com, which offer free search facilities, or you can try a subscription site such as www.ancestry.co.uk, which has a vast collection of entries transcribed from parish registers in England, Wales, Scotland and Ireland.

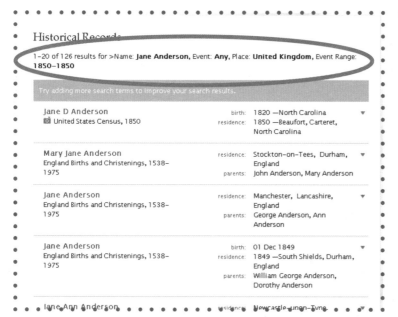

Use www.familysearch.org

1 To do a basic search, go to **www.familysearch. org**. On the home page, enter the name you want to search, plus relevant place and/or dates if known, and click **Search**. The more details you are able to enter, the more you will narrow down the search results

2 A list of results appears, containing exact matches for your entered name, as well as variations on that name. So, a search on Jane Anderson, for example, brings up Mary Jane Anderson, Jane Ann Anderson, etc. The screen indicates at the top the number of search results; to view later results, scroll down the page and click **Next**

3 In the left-hand column, you will see the names of all people related to your search, along with an indication of the source of information. In the right-hand column are further details about each person

4 If any of those listed look as though they could be the person you are searching for, click on the name to bring up another screen containing more detailed information. Alternatively, you can filter your search by clicking on any of the categories listed on the far left of your screen – such as year or place of birth, marriage or death, residence or gender

TIP
If you can't find the entry you are looking for, return to the home page and try to narrow your search down, either by selecting **Advanced Search** or, if you scroll down the screen, you can browse by location or by record collection.

5 If you click on the name you want, you will get all kinds of useful information coming up – in this case, the date and place of baptism, the names of both parents and, particularly importantly, a source film number. This is the microfilm record from which this entry was taken. You can now search for this number

in the website's library catalogue and find the location of the original parish register and transcripts or copies

6 Make a note of the source film number, then return to the home page, and select **Catalog**. In the 'Search' box, click the down arrow, and select **Film numbers**. Enter the number in the 'For' box and click **Search**

7 The screen now displays the original source for this entry and its current location. In this case, the record has been extracted from the Bishops' Transcripts for the Collegiate Church in Manchester for 1614–1851

8 Click on the source details for more information. Another screen comes up, which tells you the format(s) in which the record is available, and where you can view it. In this example, the original record and a microfilm copy are available for viewing at the Lancashire Record Office in Preston. Alternatively, for a small fee you can order the microfilm of the relevant parish register to view at your nearest LDS Family History Centre

TIPS FOR READING PARISH REGISTERS

The information contained in parish registers can be inaccurate, incomplete or difficult to decipher, so there are a number of points to bear in mind when using them to find out about your ancestors.

Spellings

Names were often spelt phonetically, especially in the earliest parish registers, so it can be difficult to know whether you have identified the correct person. If possible, try to narrow down your search by using other coordinates – for instance, names of parents or spouses, or place of residence.

Year overlap

Up to 1751, England and Wales used the Julian calendar, in which the New Year began on 25 March (Lady Day) and ended on 24 March. This means that parish registers continued beyond December into the following year. From 1 January 1752, the Gregorian calendar was adopted, but the changeover in 1751 meant that the year began on 25 March and ended on 31 December. This is worth bearing in mind if searching the registers for that year.

Latin entries

Early parish registers were often written in Latin, including names. So, if you are searching for Edward, for example, you might find him listed as Edwardus. Other Latin terms to be aware of include:

▶ Baptizatus erat – Baptised
▶ Nupti erat – Married
▶ Sepultus erat – Buried

NON-CONFORMISTS AND ROMAN CATHOLICS

If you struggle to find your ancestors mentioned in the parish registers, it could be that they were non-conformists – that is, people who broke away from the Church of England to worship in various other congregations. As the Church of England provided the only form of registration before 1837, you may still find non-conformists among the parish registers, but their appearance in the registers may be spasmodic. The reasons for this are:

TRY THIS

The best indication that your ancestors may have been non-conformist is the absence of births in the parish registers. This is because from 1743 there was a separate register for non-conformist births.

▶ At one time there was nowhere to bury ancestors other than in Anglican churchyards.
▶ From 1754 it was a legal requirement to be married in an Anglican church, except for Jews and Quakers.
▶ Some families who broke away from the Church of England to try other religions later returned, so mention within parish registers could disappear and then reappear.
▶ Some families who had broken away from the Church of England still wanted the legitimacy of having their baptisms, marriages and burials recorded.

Non-conformist religions records

Quakers (also known as the Society of Friends) were founded in the 17th century. Detailed registers exist of births and marriages, and many Quaker meeting houses had their own burial grounds.

For tracing Quaker ancestry, the best place to start is with the Friends Meeting House in London (www.quaker.org.uk/library). Their library holds a wealth of material relating to the Quaker history and faith, as well as registers of birth, marriage and deaths, lists of members (mainly from the late 18th century onwards), minutes of meetings and charity papers.

Baptists were founded in 1611. During the late 17th century they split into Particular Baptists and General Baptists, but reunited in 1891. Adult baptisms were registered. Most Baptist churches have retained their own records, so you need to know which church your ancestor attended. It is also worth contacting the Baptist Historical Society (www.baptisthistory.org.uk), which holds some records, including obituaries of Baptist ministers, as well as giving useful links.

Methodists were a part of the Church of England until the early 18th century, but became separate in the 1790s under John Wesley. Registers exist from this point onwards.

The Methodist Archives and Research Centre (MARC) was established at John Ryland's University Library, Manchester (http://library.cmsstage.manchester.ac.uk), in 1961, and holds the largest collection of books, manuscripts, private papers and records relating to Methodism.

Other major religion records

Roman Catholics were not officially recognised until the Catholic Emancipation Act of 1829 and suffered persecution for over 200 years. This has generated a wealth of records relating to the prosecution of Catholics, as well as detailed registers.

A good starting place is the Catholic National Library (www.catholic-library.org.uk), which you have to visit to access the records. This houses an extensive collection of Mission Registers, which give details of births, baptisms, confirmations, marriages, converts, deaths, obituaries and Monumental Inscriptions. They are grouped by county, so it is easier to search if you know where your Catholic ancestors lived. There is also a large collection of books and other printed matter relating to the history of Catholicism.

Jews began settling in Britain in the Middle Ages, and have been officially accepted since 1655. Some Jewish births and burials appear in parish registers, but synagogues also had their own registers.

To start tracing Jewish family history, visit JewishGen (www.jewishgen.org), which has 18 million searchable records, as well as lots of advice and useful links for further researches.

Other repositories for non-Anglican religions

The National Archives (www.nationalarchives.gov.uk) holds non-conformist registers, which were collected by the General Register Office in 1837, and some date back to the 16th century. Catholic records are also included.

The Society of Genealogists (www.sog.org.uk) holds records relating to Quakers, Baptists, Wesleyans, Congregationalists, Roman Catholics, Jews and Huguenots, including some lists of ministers, as well as copies of some non-conformist registers before 1837. You can use their website to search the online catalogue for books, but to see actual documents you need to visit the library, which is close to the City of London.

County record offices normally hold registers from 1837 onwards, so if you know which area your ancestor lived in, try the relevant CRO.

GRAVES AND INSCRIPTIONS

Gravestone inscriptions are often overlooked as a source of family history, yet they can yield all kinds of details that you may have been unable to find elsewhere. A visit to the final resting place of one of your ancestors can also be an incredibly emotional experience, as it brings you close to that ancestor in a way that no document ever can.

You are unlikely to find graves dating back to before the 17th century, as before then it was common to mark graves with a simple wooden cross, which of course won't have survived. From the 17th century onwards, it became more usual to erect stone memorials, which stood a better chance of survival.

The survival of a headstone depends greatly on the materials used; limestone is soft and therefore weathers easily, but slate is harder and more likely to have withstood the elements.

What a gravestone can tell you

The amount of information recorded on a headstone obviously varies greatly, but even just a name and date of death can clarify details you have already discovered, or give clues for further research. Many gravestones, of course, give much more detail than this. It is not unusual to find several generations buried in one grave, or to find several family graves grouped together in a churchyard, and between them they can enable you to fill in some gaps in your family tree.

Details you may get from gravestones include:
- ▶ Deceased's full name.
- ▶ Date (or sometimes just the year) of birth.
- ▶ Place of birth.
- ▶ Age at death.
- ▶ Cause of death.
- ▶ Occupation.
- ▶ Military service.
- ▶ Any official titles, such as Captain or Doctor.
- ▶ Letters after the name, indicating a qualification.
- ▶ Quotes from the Bible, poems or other literary works, indicating a favourite text.
- ▶ Decorations and/or symbols, indicating special interests or religious denomination.
- ▶ Names of other members of the family, who may or may not be buried in the same grave – if you are lucky, you may find details for two or three generations.

BE CAREFUL

Dates on gravestones are not always reliable, because the memorial may have been erected some time after the death, especially if the family was not wealthy and took a while to find the necessary funds. So always check dates against other sources if you can.

Search for a grave online using findagrave.com

1 Go to **www.findagrave.com** and under the 'Find Graves' heading click **Search 67 million grave records**

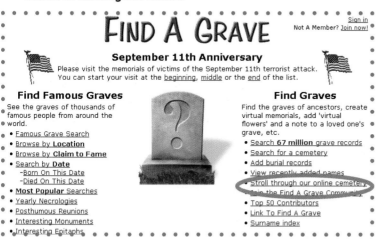

2 Enter as much information as you know about your ancestor, and click **Search** or press **Enter**. If you don't know the exact years of birth and death, you can put in approximate years to help narrow your search

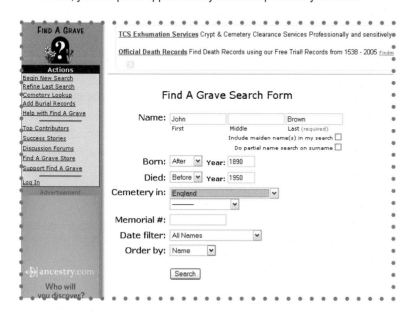

TRY THIS

It's best to enter an After date for Born; if you put in a Before date, you will get a huge list of results, unless you have a really unusual surname.

3 You will now have a list of people matching your search criteria, together with details of grave or cemetery locations

4 Click on the location that seems most likely for your ancestor

Blight, Diana b. 1884 d. Nov. 16, 1958	St John Graveyard Westerhope Tyne and Wear England
Boyd, Joseph Henry b. 1869 d. Feb. 5, 1940	St John Graveyard Westerhope Tyne and Wear England
Briggs, Elizabeth b. 1887 d. Mar. 27, 1941	St John Graveyard Westerhope Tyne and Wear England
Brooks, Elizabeth Ann b. 1841 d. Mar. 4, 1915	St John Graveyard Westerhope Tyne and Wear England
Brown, Grace Ann b. 1868 d. May 21, 1942	St John Graveyard Westerhope Tyne and Wear England
Brown, John b. 1899 d. Aug. 16, 1938	St John Graveyard Westerhope Tyne and Wear England
Bulford, Alfred D. b. 1916 d. Jan. 26, 1979	St John Graveyard Westerhope Tyne and Wear England

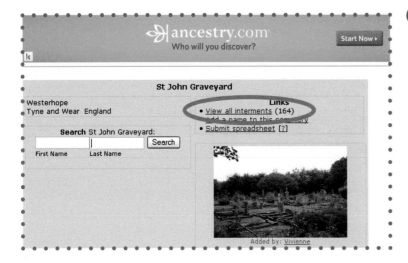

ancestry.com
Who will you discover?

Start Now ▸

St John Graveyard

Westerhope
Tyne and Wear England

Links
- View all interments (164)
- Add a name to this cemetery
- Submit spreadsheet [?]

Search St John Graveyard:

First Name	Last Name

Search

Added by: Vivienne

5 You will get another screen giving you a link that will take you to a full list of interments at that site

6 Scroll down to your ancestor, and click on his name. This will give you further details about him – in this case, his year of birth, exact date of death and gravestone inscription. You now have some details to add to your family tree, if you haven't already got them, and also know where to visit the grave yourself

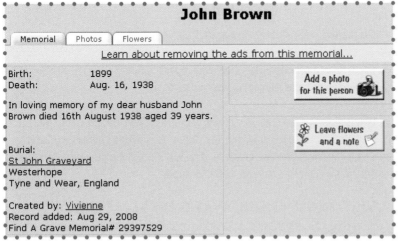

John Brown

| Memorial | Photos | Flowers |

Learn about removing the ads from this memorial...

Birth: 1899
Death: Aug. 16, 1938

In loving memory of my dear husband John Brown died 16th August 1938 aged 39 years.

Add a photo for this person

Leave flowers and a note

Burial:
St John Graveyard
Westerhope
Tyne and Wear, England

Created by: Vivienne
Record added: Aug 29, 2008
Find A Grave Memorial# 29397529

7 In some cases, you will get extra details – in this example, if you click on the name Grace Ann Brown, you get not only details of Grace's birth and death, but also information about her husband, which gives you his date of death and enables you to work out his probable year of birth (which has to be 1866, unless he was born after 19 December and died just short of his 82nd birthday)

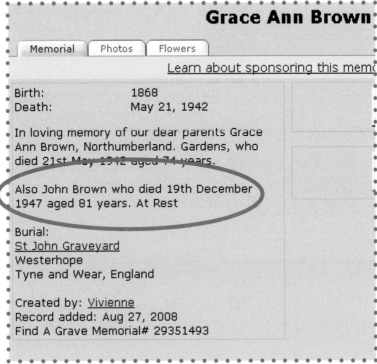

Grace Ann Brown

| Memorial | Photos | Flowers |

Learn about sponsoring this memo

Birth: 1868
Death: May 21, 1942

In loving memory of our dear parents Grace Ann Brown, Northumberland. Gardens, who died 21st May, 1942 aged 74 years.

Also John Brown who died 19th December 1947 aged 81 years. At Rest

Burial:
St John Graveyard
Westerhope
Tyne and Wear, England

Created by: Vivienne
Record added: Aug 27, 2008
Find A Grave Memorial# 29351493

BE CAREFUL

Don't assume that everyone mentioned on a gravestone or other memorial is necessarily buried there. Sometimes it's obvious who was actually interred in the grave, but this is not always the case, so you may need to check the burial location for other names listed.

Other ways to locate a grave

The National Burial Index (see page 78) will give you the exact location of your ancestor's grave, and covers Anglican and non-conformist graveyards and cemeteries.

Newspaper death notices usually state where a burial was to take place.

Obituaries (see pages 71–2) may indicate where a burial took place.

Local record offices usually hold church and cemetery records, so it's worth contacting the one relevant to your ancestor.

War heroes If you know your ancestor died in action, try searching the website for the Commonwealth War Graves Commission (www.cwgc.org). This is the largest online database of people killed during the two world wars, and most records include the burial location.

VISITING A CHURCHYARD OR CEMETERY

Before you go, check your local record office to see whether they have a plot map for the burial ground you are visiting. This can save you a lot of time once you get to the graveyard, as you will know exactly where to go.

At the churchyard or cemetery

1 Make sure you take a photograph of the grave and, if possible, a close-up of the inscription. These will make interesting additions to your family records folder, and will be particularly valuable if the headstone is later destroyed or removed, or becomes illegible

TIP
When visiting a churchyard, make sure you take your camera, a notebook and pen with you.

2 Copy the inscription into your notebook as well, as a backup. If parts of the inscription are illegible, just leave blanks for now – you may be able to work out or discover the missing information later on. It's also possible that the inscription has already been transcribed and is available online (see Monumental Inscriptions, pages 94–5). Even an incomplete inscription can supply you with some details to add to your family tree, and give you clues for further research

3 Look at other graves nearby as they could mark the final resting places of other members of the same family, some of whom you may be unaware of. This can help fill in missing details on your family tree, and perhaps clarify relationships within the family

Inside the church

If you are visiting a churchyard, it's always worth looking inside the church as well, especially if this was your ancestor's local church for many years. There may well be more clues about your family waiting to be discovered.

▶ If your ancestor was a war hero, you may well find him listed on a roll of honour, along with other members of the family. This can be very revealing – you may already know, for example, that Great Uncle George was killed in action at Gallipoli, but you may see someone with the same surname mentioned in the same roll of honour, perhaps a brother or cousin. Now you have some more details for your family tree, and a new avenue to explore.

▶ If your ancestor was the rector, he will almost certainly be included on a list inside the church, with the relevant dates. You may also discover that an ancestor of yours was a churchwarden or some other parish official, again with relevant dates.

▶ Wealthy and influential families were usually buried and/or commemorated inside the church. Memorials include brass plaques or stones set into the wall or floor, stained glass windows (usually if someone did something particularly noteworthy) or, if the family was very wealthy, a large stone tomb with effigies and elaborate decoration, often containing several members of the same family.

TRY THIS

A gravestone can sometimes give you as much information as a certificate – so you might save yourself the cost of purchasing some certificates!

Next step

To further your researches for a member of the clergy or the armed forces, see pages 130–2 and 137–40.

▶ Before Civil Registration

HOW TO READ A HEADSTONE

In addition to the inscription, there are other features on a headstone that can tell you a bit more about your ancestors. Things to look for include:

Type of stone used Local stone was the cheapest option, while imported stone was more expensive and therefore indicative of a wealthier family.

Style of headstone Headstone shapes changed over the centuries, from small, crude stones with little inscription before the 17th century, to the larger, more elaborately shaped and carved headstones of the 18th and 19th centuries. In the 17th century, it was also common practice to place the headstone facing away from the grave, rather than towards it.

Decoration Similarly, decorative carving was expensive, so the more elaborate the decoration on a headstone, the wealthier the family was likely to have been. Other forms of decoration include side columns on the headstone, the use of kerbstones around the grave, and the inclusion of a stone body over the grave.

Position The south and east sides of the churchyard were the most popular locations, so anyone buried there is likely to have had greater status and influence than those buried elsewhere. The north side was the least popular, and often reserved for the less 'desirable' inhabitants of the parish – illegitimates, the unbaptised, suicides and non-conformists.

Symbols These were popular from the 18th century onwards. Some you may come across include:

TRY THIS
The changing styles and sizes of gravestones can help you date the grave – useful if the inscription is hard to read.

▶ Weeping figures, willows, urns and garlands were popular in the 18th century, all symbolising grief.
▶ Religious symbols became more popular in the Victorian era and included sacrificial lambs, clasped hands and angels or cherubs. Crosses also became increasingly popular, now they were no longer associated exclusively with Roman Catholics.
▶ Tools or other relevant symbols indicating a person's trade.

What if you can't find an ancestor's grave?
There could be any number of reasons for not being able to find an ancestor's grave. Possibilities include:

▶ The grave has been destroyed by wartime bombing, vandalism or nature (lichen is a common problem on gravestones).

- The headstone is so old or has become so badly weathered that it is no longer legible, and therefore unidentifiable.
- The grave has been moved elsewhere by the local authority, in which case the county record office should be able to tell you its new location.
- The gravestone has been removed from its original location for health and safety reasons, and stacked against the exterior walls – so it's worth looking there if you are convinced that your ancestor is buried in that particular churchyard or cemetery.
- Your ancestor might have been a pauper and therefore buried in an unmarked, communal grave.

TIP

If you draw a blank on finding a particular ancestor's grave, it's best not to waste too much time on it – accept that the grave no longer exists, and focus on other resources.

before civil registration

TRANSCRIPTIONS OF MONUMENTAL INSCRIPTIONS

Visiting graveyards is a rewarding experience, but what if you are unable to visit, or the graveyard no longer exists? No problem – many Monumental Inscriptions (MIs), as they are officially known, have been transcribed and are stored in a variety of repositories.

Where to find MI transcriptions

Local record offices often hold transcriptions, especially where graves have been removed or destroyed. The Genuki website (www.genuki.org.uk) gives details of record offices for each county, or you can just use a search engine to find the relevant county or parish.

The Society of Genealogists has one of the largest collections of transcriptions, arranged in their library by county. You can search their catalogue online (www.sog.org.uk/sogcat/access) to see which books they have available on the subject, but will need to visit the library in person to view the transcriptions.

Most family history societies have ongoing transcription projects, with the results published in booklets or on CD. Visit the Federation of Family History Societies website (www.ffhs.org.uk) for a list of societies in England, Wales and Ireland; for Scottish family history societies visit The Scottish Association of Family History Societies (www.safhs.org.uk).

Find MI transcriptions online

There are a number of websites with MI transcriptions, but you may need to search more than one as most are ongoing projects that are far from complete.

www.findmypast.co.uk has the largest collection of online transcriptions, currently covering 11 English counties and one Welsh county (Glamorgan). The site is free to search, but you need to pay to view records and transcripts.

The Gravestone Photographic Resource (www.gravestonephotos.com) is another ongoing project, which records images and information from monuments from all over the world, including some that no longer exist. The site includes headstones, floor slabs, plaques and stained glass windows.

Local websites for counties in England, Wales, Ireland and Scotland are worth investigating – search www.genuki.org.uk for details for each county. For example, a search under 'Cemeteries' in the Norfolk pages reveals links to four websites containing information on Monumental Inscriptions in the county.

Transcriptions for some Scottish gravestones can be found at www. scotlandsfamily.com, but again coverage is patchy; some counties are well covered, while others are not covered at all.

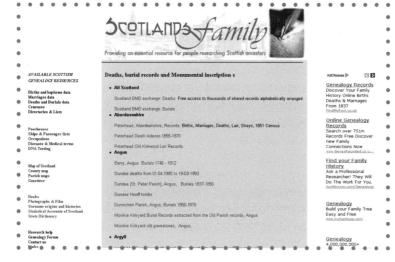

TIP

Although obtaining transcriptions of MIs can be very useful, do try to visit the original grave yourself at some point if you can, as errors can occur, especially when people are deciphering inscriptions that are badly worn.

For Irish transcriptions, try www.historyfromheadstones.com, which covers 800 graveyards in the counties of Antrim, Armagh, Down, Fermanagh, Londonderry and Tyrone. Searching is free, but you need to pay to view records. You can also try www.rootsireland.ie, but again you need to pay to view.

WILLS PROVED IN ECCLESIASTICAL COURTS

Wills from 1858 are covered on pages 68–70, when proving wills in England and Wales became the responsibility of the state. But what happened before 1858?

Pre-1858 wills were under the jurisdiction of the ecclesiastical courts. There were two central courts – the Prerogative Court of Canterbury (PCC) and the Prerogative Court of York (PYC) – along with around 250 lower ecclesiastical courts, which were the Archdeacon, Bishop diocesan and Peculiar courts. A 'peculiar' court was one that came under the jurisdiction of a different archdeaconry or bishop's diocese to the one in which it was located. In most cases, records from the peculiar courts can be found in the record office of their geographical archdeaconry or diocese, but are sometimes found in manorial records (see pages 167–8).

A 'will' refers to real estate (property), whereas a 'testament' refers to personal goods such as jewellery, clothing, furniture and other household items, tools of a particular trade, animals and stocks and shares.

What a will can tell you
- ▶ Full name of the deceased.
- ▶ Occupation of the deceased.
- ▶ Parish and county in which the deceased was living at the time of death.
- ▶ Names of other family members, and their relationship to the deceased and to each other.
- ▶ The omission of family members may indicate a rift in the family – an intriguing puzzle that you might never be able to solve!
- ▶ Date of probate (which can be up to three years after the date of death, sometimes longer).

Where to find wills
If you know which parish your ancestor was living in at the time of death, this should help determine which ecclesiastical court had jurisdiction over the will. This in turn should lead you to the appropriate repository.

If a person's property was held in one place, the will would have been proved at an Archdeacon's, Bishop's or Peculiar court. Any surviving records are now held by the relevant diocesan or county record office.

If your ancestor was wealthy and/or had property in more than one place, or died abroad or at sea leaving property in England or Wales, the will would have been proved at one of the Prerogative courts.

Indexes to most wills in England can be viewed at The National Archives at Kew (www.nationalarchives.gov.uk), LDS family history centres (www.familysearch.org), the Society of Genealogists (www.sog.org.uk) and some record offices.

The Prerogative Court of Canterbury (PCC) had jurisdiction over the south of England and Wales. Original copies of wills proved between 1384 and 1858 are held by The National Archives at Kew (www.nationalarchives.gov.uk), and they have all been indexed. During the English Civil War (1643–46), wills coming under the jurisdiction of the Prerogative Court of Canterbury were proved in Oxford rather than London. Some of these wills were later proved for a second time in London, but those that weren't are held in a separate collection at The National Archives, catalogue reference PROB 10/639-642. You can search the indexes online (see pages 108–14).

The Prerogative Court of York
(PCY) had jurisdiction over northern England and wills proved between 1389 and 1858 are held at the Borthwick Institute in York (www.york.ac.uk/library/borthwick), which also holds wills proved in the lower ecclesiastical courts for the region.

The National Library of Wales
(www.llgc.org.uk) stores wills proved in Welsh ecclesiastical courts. The library also has an index of wills.

TIP

A useful guide to start you off on your search is the book *Wills and Probate Records* by Karen Grannum and Nigel Taylor (The National Archives, 2009), which covers all national sources for wills and probate records.

before civil registration

SEARCH FOR WILLS ONLINE

Searching online can be a good way to start tracking down your ancestors' wills and there can be no better to place to start than The National Archives.

Use The National Archives to search for a will

1 Go to **www.nationalarchives.gov.uk/documentsonline** and select **Wills and death duties** under the 'Quick links' heading

2 On the next screen, click **Search** under the 'Prerogative Court of Canterbury wills (PROB 11)' heading

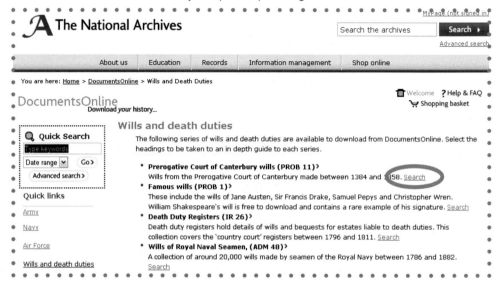

3 You are then taken to a search screen, where you can search by first or last name, occupation or place of residence. Add other keywords and a date range. Click **Search**

4 A search for John Anderson, for example, throws up 171 documents. You can now either scroll down to find your ancestor, or narrow your search further by selecting **Refine search** and adding any additional information

5 If you can see your ancestor in the list, select **See details**, and a screen will come up with all sorts of useful information – including the catalogue reference, the image reference and format and source of the original document. Most importantly, if you are sure this is the document you want, you can purchase a copy for £3.50 by clicking **Add to shopping**

Other useful places to look

Estate Duty or Death Duty Registers From 1796, when a Legacy Duty came into force, registers were compiled of wills on which duty was payable. The annual indexes covering 1796–1903, along with surviving registers, are held by The National Archives, where you can view copies on microfilm. There is also a limited selection of wills online at www.nationalarchives.gov.uk/documentsonline/wills.asp, where you can see wills of famous people, including Shakespeare, Nelson and Jane Austen, as well as those of Royal Naval seamen. The research guide 'Wills and Probate Records' is also worth consulting at www.nationalarchives.gov.uk/records/research-guides/wills-and-probate-records.htm.

Will abstracts Some record offices hold published abstracts of wills, which strip away the legal jargon and focus on the essential information. These can be more user-friendly than the actual wills, but, as always, check them against the original documents as errors and omissions do occur.

POOR LAW RECORDS

Various laws existed from the 16th century onwards to ensure that those who fell into hardship were given financial and practical support, funded by compulsory contributions from ratepayers (known as poor rates). These generated a variety of records that can be of great value to family historians, whether your ancestor was a ratepayer or in receipt of poor relief.

Before 1834, the responsibility for looking after the poor lay with individual parishes, and was administered by the Overseers of the Poor, who met monthly and kept records of the collection and distribution of funds. Overseers were nominated annually and included churchwardens and local householders.

The Poor Law Amendment Act of 1834 saw parishes grouped together into Poor Law Unions, which were headed by elected Guardians of the Poor. Each Poor Law Union was required to provide a workhouse – a dreaded institution, to which the able-bodied poor were sent.

In 1930, poor relief became the responsibility of county and borough councils, under the direction of the Ministry of Health, and remained so until the introduction of the Welfare State in 1948.

What Poor Law records can tell you

▶ Confirmation of ancestors' home parishes.
▶ Whether they were in receipt of poor relief and, if so, for how long – this can help you trace your family's rise and/or decline in fortunes.
▶ Which trade(s) your ancestors were involved in, if any.
▶ Whether your ancestors were clergymen or if they held any other official parish offices.
▶ Details of any apprenticeships undertaken by your ancestors.

Find a Poor Law record

Poor Law records were originally kept in a lockable iron chest, alongside the parish registers, and so came to be known as Parish Chest material. You can now find this material in county record offices.

The Workhouse website (www.workhouses.org.uk) lists repositories for workhouse and other Poor Law records, as well as giving a detailed history of the Poor Laws.

The National Archives holds a large collection of Poor Law documents from 1834 onwards. Some records have been digitised and these are free to search and download (series ref. MH12). This only covers some parts of the country, but it is worth a look in case it includes areas relevant to you.

Poor Law records

Overseers' Account Books contain details of payments made to the poor to cover such things as rent, clothing, food, medical expenses and burials, and include names of recipients. If your ancestor received poor relief, you should find his/her name included here.

Churchwardens' accounts contained details of all parish expenses, including payments to the poor, as well as details of services and goods provided to the parish. They can be a useful backup to the Overseers' accounts, by providing missing details or simply corroborating facts. They are also useful if your ancestor was a local tradesman.

Parish rate books were compiled annually, and list all individuals who paid local poor rates. This effectively gives you an annual census of all heads of households within a particular parish, other than those in receipt of poor relief, and this can help to confirm or determine life spans and your family's movements between parishes, if any.

Settlement certificates were introduced by the Settlement Act of 1662, which stated that every individual should 'belong' to a particular parish. This enabled authorities to determine which parish was responsible for a person's welfare if they became ill or destitute. Until 1697, only migrant workers were required to have settlement certificates, but thereafter anybody deemed likely to need poor relief was required to have one. Information on a settlement certificate includes:

- ▶ Name of the certificate holder.
- ▶ Name of the parish to which the person 'belonged' (therefore a useful way of determining your ancestor's home parish).
- ▶ Signatures of the Overseers of the Poor, the Churchwardens and two witnesses (useful if your ancestor held any of these offices).

Settlement examinations were undertaken by magistrates if someone fell on hard times while away from their home parish, and could result in a Removal Order to return them to that parish, which would be responsible for their welfare. Documents recording settlement examinations are rare, but if you are lucky enough to find one for your ancestor, you could find lots of extra useful biographical details.

Vestry minutes were kept from the 14th century until 1834, and included details of administration and maintenance of parish schools, almshouses, workhouses, the church and poor relief.

Workhouse records give details of admissions and discharges, along with other useful information such as dates of birth and death. Workhouses existed as far back as the 16th century, but few records survive from before 1834. Workhouse inmates were included in the census returns, so you can cross-reference any information discovered in workhouse records with the appropriate census returns (see pages 26–46). The Workhouse website (www.workhouses.org. uk) gives lots of useful information about workhouses, including workhouse locations, life in the workhouse and much more.

Parish Apprentices

Parish officials were responsible for apprenticing children of paupers to local parishioners and tradesmen, which usually meant the children became farm labourers or domestic servants. An apprenticeship indenture was the legal document binding a child to a master, normally paid for by the parents but, in the case of paupers, by the Overseer of the Poor. Many of these indentures have survived and include:

- ► Master's name, address and occupation.
- ► Child's name.
- ► Dates of apprenticeship.
- ► Whether the apprenticeship was completed.
- ► In some cases, the names and address of the child's parents.

Next step

For more information about apprenticeships and where to find records, see pages 119–21.

USING ARCHIVES

By reading and following all the steps in this chapter, you will find out how to:

▶ **Identify the best archive or research centre to visit**

▶ **Plan your visit to the archives**

▶ **Get the most out of your visit**

▶ Using Archives

CHOOSE A REPOSITORY

Despite the wealth of genealogy information available online these days, there will come a point in your research when you will need to visit a library or record office, either to check facts gleaned so far against original documents, or because the documents you need are not yet available online.

Visiting libraries and archives can be a very pleasurable thing to do. Researching online may be quick and convenient, but it can be exciting handling original documents (where you're allowed to do so), looking at old books and feeling that you're in a place with like-minded people, as well as having experienced staff on hand to help.

It can be daunting, though, visiting archives for the first time, so this chapter will smooth your path for you.

Local library and studies centre

Your local library is usually a good place to start, especially if you are researching family in your area.

In the main library you will find books relating to the history and geography of the area, which can give you an idea of what the place was like during the times of your ancestors. They can also be a good source for finding out useful facts and dates.

The local studies section of a library is usually separate, and holds records relating to the area. Typically, this includes copies of:
▶ Parish registers.
▶ The BMD index.
▶ Census returns.
▶ Local council records.
▶ Copies of local newspapers.

Some of this will almost certainly be on microfilm/fiche. The local studies centre may also have access to some national records, in particular the BMD index, so this can be a good starting point for researching ancestors outside the area.

You don't normally need a ticket for local libraries and studies centres, unless you want to borrow books from the main library.

County record offices and diocesan record offices

Increasingly, the old county and diocesan record offices are being amalgamated with other local archives to form one vast record collection. If you're not sure what official title your local county collection has been given, you can simply type the name of the old record office into a search engine and it will automatically take you to the new archive.

For example, typing 'Oxfordshire County Record Office' into Google throws up this list of results. Click on the first entry and the record office explains it has now been merged with Oxfordshire Studies and Oxfordshire Health Archives to form the new Oxfordshire History Centre.

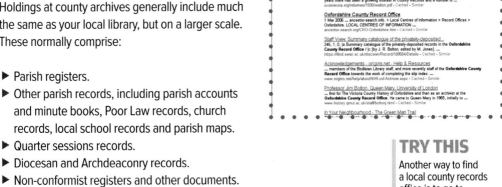

Holdings at county archives generally include much the same as your local library, but on a larger scale. These normally comprise:

▶ Parish registers.
▶ Other parish records, including parish accounts and minute books, Poor Law records, church records, local school records and parish maps.
▶ Quarter sessions records.
▶ Diocesan and Archdeaconry records.
▶ Non-conformist registers and other documents.
▶ Probate records.
▶ Records of local businesses.
▶ Local authority records.
▶ Local newspapers.
▶ Street and trade directories.
▶ Maps and plans.
▶ Photographs.
▶ Oral history.
▶ CD-ROMS.

The majority of local archives provide free access to subscription websites, such as www.ancestry.co.uk and www.findmypast.co.uk.

TRY THIS

Another way to find a local county records office is to go to www.genuki.org.uk. See page 142 to find out how to use the website.

▶ Using Archives

Most local archives are still organised according to the old county boundaries, so you need to know which county your place of interest was in before 1974. In some cases, though, records might have been transferred from one county archive to another, so it is worth checking this before your visit.

Most local archives belong to the County Archives Record Network (CARN), which means that you will need a reader's ticket to access original records. The ticket is valid for four years at all CARN record offices in the country. Tickets are usually issued free on production of two passport-size photographs and evidence of your address and signature. You don't need a ticket to access secondary sources, such as printed transcripts and indexes.

If you are unable to visit your local archives, you will find at least some of their holdings are accessible online, and most also run enquiry services.

Family History Centres
The Church of Jesus Christ of Latter-Day Saints (LDS) has established a worldwide network of Family History Centres, and anyone is welcome to use these centres free of charge. To find a Family History Centre near you, use the search facility on their website, www.familysearch.org/eng.

Records at the Family History Centres include censuses, BMD records, military records, probate and court records, and records relating to migration and naturalisation, covering the whole world and in some cases going back to the 13th century. Many of these records are also searchable online.

The National Library of Wales
Not just the national library of Wales, this is also the principal archive for researching Welsh family history. You can search the catalogue at http://cat.llgc.org.uk. Holdings include church records, archives of landed estates and national institutions, court records, maps, photographs and historical and literary manuscripts.

National Records of Scotland (NRS)
Scotland's main repository for genealogy records, the NRS was formed in April 2011 from the merger of The National Archives of Scotland and the General Register Office. This will bring together censuses, parish registers and civil registers from the General Register Office for Scotland (www.gro-scotland.gov.uk) and government, local authority, court and church records, legal registers, records of nationalised industries and transport, private family papers, records of businesses, maps and plans from The National Archives of

Scotland (www.nas.gov.uk). You will be able to use these websites until the new NRS website is up and running.

The British Library
The British Library (www.bl.uk) is a treasure trove of books, manuscripts and documents, with a range of searchable online catalogues. The library includes a number of specialist libraries. The areas of most interest to family historians include:

The Newspaper Library at Colindale
Avenue This is a vast collection of British and overseas newspapers, magazines, comics and trade journals dating back to the 17th century. This is the place to go for those elusive obituaries, birth and marriage announcements, death notices, theatre reviews and much more that you have been unable to locate elsewhere. You can search the digital catalogue at http://newspapers. bl.uk/blcs/, but will need to subscribe to gain full access.

The Sound Archive at St Pancras
includes an oral history collection, which is researchable online at www.bl.uk/nsa.

The main library at Euston Street is a
copyright library so it has a copy of every book published, so anything you've been unable to track down in your local library will be here.

Other copyright libraries
The British Library is one of five copyright libraries in the UK. The other four are:
▶ Bodleian Library, Oxford: www.bodleian.ox.ac.uk/bodley
▶ The National Library of Scotland, Edinburgh: www.nls.uk
▶ The National Library of Wales, Aberystwyth: www.llgc.org.uk
▶ Trinity College, Dublin: www.tcd.ie/Library

⊳ Using Archives

THE NATIONAL ARCHIVES

The National Archives at Kew was formed between 2003 and 2006 from the merger of the Public Record Office, the Royal Commission on Historic Manuscripts, Her Majesty's Stationery Office and the Office of Public Sector Information. It is now the principal repository for the United Kingdom, with over a thousand years' worth of government and public records. Its holdings include:

▶ General Register Office records, including census returns and registers of non-parochial births, marriages and deaths.
▶ Court records.
▶ Records from government departments, including the Armed Forces, Metropolitan Police, Inland Revenue, Colonial Office and many more.
▶ Records from various businesses and organisations, including canal and railway companies.

Explore The National Archives online

To find out more about the National Archives' holdings, you can look at the catalogue online.

1 Go to **www.nationalarchives.gov.uk** and click **The Catalogue** from the 'Quick Links' on the right of your screen

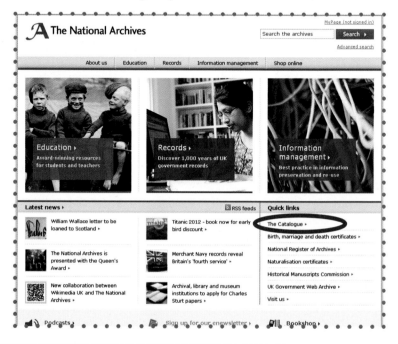

❷ From here you can either start searching the Catalogue or, if you are new to the site, it is worth clicking on **More about what's in the catalogue** to get a feel for the scope of records available. This explains more about the contents of the catalogue, and how it works

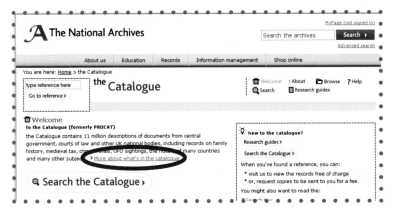

❸ Useful sections to click on here include **Structure of the Catalogue** and **Popular codes for government departments**, both of which explain more about how the catalogue works and how to interpret search results

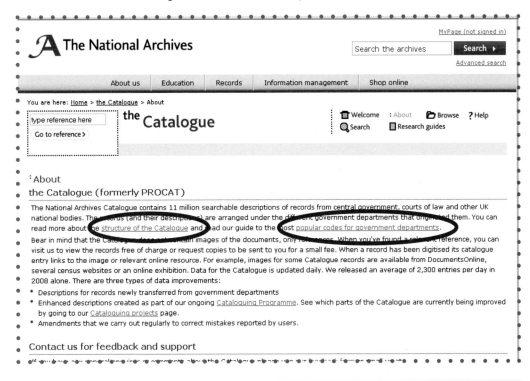

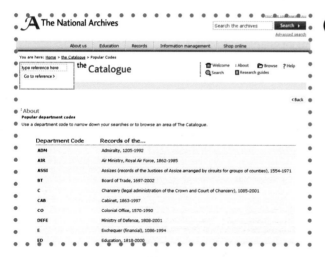

4 The 'Department Codes' are particularly useful, as you can use these to narrow down your search for records. Within each department you will find series references. HO, for example, is the department code for the Home Office and within that department you will find different series of documents. HO 107, for example, is the series reference for the 1841 and 1851 censuses. See page 112 for a complete list of department codes

5 The 'Research Guides' are also very helpful. From the main Catalogue page (as shown at Step 2), click **Research Guides**, and then select from the alphabetical list

6 Another useful section to look in on The National Archives website is the 'Records' section. From the home page, click **Records** to bring up a range of useful links and online tutorials

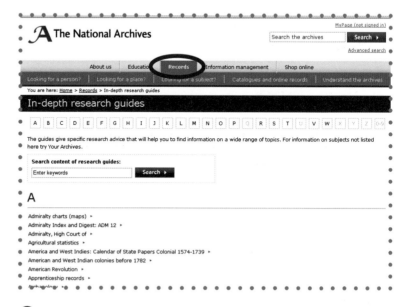

7 Finally, there is the link to 'Catalogues and online records', which includes links to other websites and archives

Searching online for a record not held at Kew

If you try searching for something on the website that isn't held at Kew, the website will direct you to the correct repository.

1 Suppose, for example, you are interested in birth, marriage and death certificates. Select this from the 'Quick Links' list on the home page (as shown in Step 1 on page 108). On the next screen, select the required location, and then click **Next**

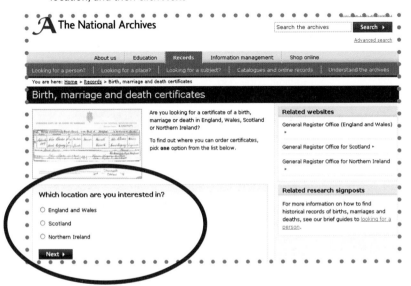

2 The next screen directs you to the correct repository – in this example, the General Register Office for Scotland – and helpfully gives you a link to the website

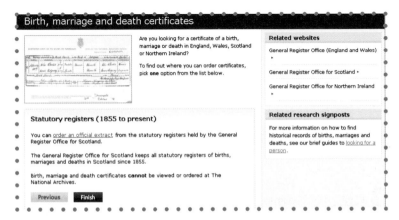

▶ Using Archives

The National Archives department codes

As an overview, this is the list of department codes and the material that each one holds. This information, combined with the powerful search tools on The National Archives website means you have a vast array of knowledge at your fingertips.

ADM	Admiralty, 1205–1992
AIR	Air Ministry, Royal Air Force, 1862–1985
ASSI	Assizes (records of the Justices of Assize arranged by circuits for groups of counties), 1554–1971
BT	Board of Trade, 1697–2002
C	Chancery (legal administration of the Crown and Court of Chancery), 1085–2001
CAB	Cabinet, 1863–1997
CO	Colonial Office, 1570–1990
DEFE	Ministry of Defence, 1808–2001
E	Exchequer (financial), 1086–1994
ED	Education, 1818–2000
FCO	Foreign and Commonwealth Office, 1950–1990
FO	Foreign Office, 1567–2002
HO	Home Office, 1700–2002
HW	Government Communications Headquarters (records relating to interception of enemy communications and security of government electronic communications), 1914–1978
IR	Inland Revenue, Boards of Stamps, Taxes, Excise (including Tithe maps and death duty registers), 1513–1999
KB	Court of King's Bench (relating to litigation in which the state has an interest), 1194–1987
KV	Records of the Security Service, 1905–1953
LAB	Labour and Employment Departments, 1836–1995
MEPO	Metropolitan Police Office, 1803–1995
RAIL	Railway and Canal Companies, 1634–1982
RG	General Register Office (including census of population and some non-parochial births, marriages and death registers), 1567–1999
SC	Special Collections (including Court Rolls, Papal Bulls, Ancient Petitions and Seals), 12th century–20th century
SP	State Paper Office and Secretaries of State, 1231–c.1888
WO	War Office (including service records and regimental war diaries), 1568–1996
T	Treasury, 1547–1996

Search The National Archives online database

1 From the home page, **www.nationalarchives.gov.uk**, select **The Catalogue** from the 'Quick Links' on the right

2 If you want to browse a specific series, enter the reference in the box at the top left of your screen and click **Go to reference**. This will take you to the relevant section. From there you can browse that section of the Catalogue, which will tell you which records are available and give you the necessary links

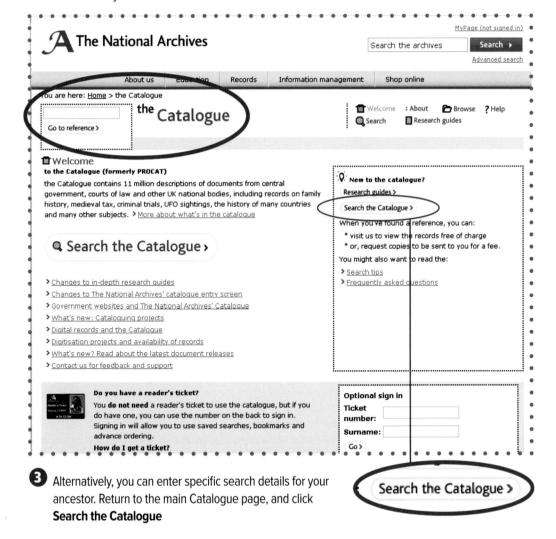

3 Alternatively, you can enter specific search details for your ancestor. Return to the main Catalogue page, and click **Search the Catalogue**

4 Enter as many known details about your ancestor as you can, and click **Search**

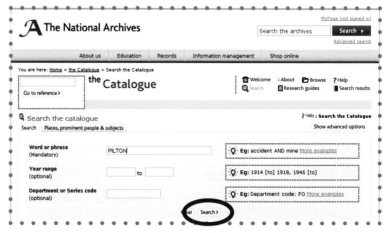

5 Hopefully, you will get a list of entries relating to the details entered. Scroll down to see if any of these are (or could be) your ancestor, and click on the relevant entry. For example, a search on Pilton in the WO series produced 29 results. Selecting Thomas Lewis, born in Pilton, Somerset, revealed that he served in the 46th Foot Regiment, and was discharged at the age of 35

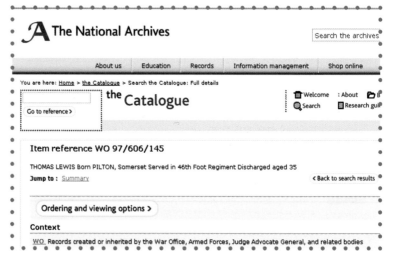

6 Click **Ordering and viewing options**. If you are sure this is your ancestor, you can go through to a screen allowing you to download the full record for a fee

MAKE THE MOST OF A VISIT TO AN ARCHIVE

Visiting an archive or library for the first time can seem daunting, but with a bit of preparation you can ensure that you get the most out of your visit.

Before you go
- Find out whether your chosen repository has introductory talks and/or guided tours. Most do this and it's a very helpful way of getting to know the layout and contents of the archive. This will save you time when you visit.
- It might sound obvious, but don't forget to check the opening times – not all archives are open every day, and their opening/closing times might vary from one day to another.
- Book in advance. Most archives require you to do this anyway, but even for those that don't it's worth booking in advance as they can get very busy. It's particularly important to do so if you want to book a computer terminal or microfiche reader.
- If you know which documents you want to look at, phone and ask in advance so that staff can have them ready for you when you arrive. If you know the document reference numbers, this will be a great help to the staff, but don't worry if you don't – they will still be retrievable.
- Make a list of the things you want to look up when you're there as this will save time and stop you getting sidetracked.

What to take with you
- Several pencils – you won't be allowed to use ink pens, as they can permanently damage the documents, nor can you take pencil sharpeners or erasers into the archives.
- A large notebook – at least A5.
- Loose change for things such as the photocopying machine, lockers, vending machine and car park.
- Food and drink because not all archives have cafés, and there may not be anywhere close by to go for refreshments. Most archives will at least provide a seating area where you can eat and drink.
- If you want to get a reader's ticket, you need to take two passport-size photos with you together with some identification that shows your home address and signature.

At the archive
- Collect any leaflets available as they are very useful guides to the archives and the best ways of using them.
- Don't be afraid to ask staff if you're not sure about anything – they are there to help.

TRY THIS

If you are visiting a library or record office, print off just the section of family tree relevant to your research. That will stop you from getting sidetracked.

▶ When making notes from documents, don't be tempted to abbreviate or expand words, or omit anything as you might find it hard to decipher your notes later on. Copy everything accurately, word for word.

▶ Don't be tempted to 'correct' anything that looks wrong, such as spellings or dates. If they turn out to be correct after all, you could find yourself wasting a lot of time.

▶ Don't make assumptions about what you see. For example, don't assume that 'Ed' is short for 'Edward', as it could be 'Edmund'.

▶ If there's anything you can't decipher, leave a gap and carry on. You might be able to fill the gap through other research, or it could turn out to be unimportant.

▶ Make sure you write neatly – difficult when you're getting tired, but it can save you time and effort later on.

▶ Make a note of the reference number for each record you view. This makes it easier to retrieve if you need to see it again.

▶ If you use a book, make sure you note its location, as well as the title, author, publisher, publication date, the edition, and relevant page numbers.

▶ If you access a website, either print it out or make a careful note of the website address so that you can easily find it again.

▶ Handle original documents and microfilm/fiche sheets with extreme care. If you are worried about handling rare and valuable documents, ask a member of staff for advice.

▶ Don't try to do too much in one day, as looking at old documents and computer screens for a long time is tiring. Instead, you might need to make several visits.

OCCUPATIONS

By reading and following all the steps in this chapter, you will find out how to:

▶ **Learn about your ancestors' working lives**

▶ **Trace them through occupational records**

▶ **Investigate your military ancestors**

▶ Occupations

People were prone to exaggeration when describing their occupations in official forms such as census returns, parish registers and civil registration certificates. Spelling errors and hard-to-decipher handwriting were also common. So you may need to do a bit of creative thinking. A man describing himself as a farmer, for instance, could have been a humble agricultural labourer.

DELVE DEEPER INTO OCCUPATIONS

As you will have seen from previous chapters, civil and parish registers, census returns, wills, obituaries and family memorabilia can all tell you what your ancestors did for a living. Delving deeper into those occupations by looking at relevant registers, business records and trade union records, for example, can give you a fascinating glimpse into your ancestors' lives, as well as revealing or clarifying essential details for your family tree.

Sometimes an employment record will give you more details about your ancestor than, for example, a parish register. Many trades and professions were passed down from one generation to another, so records can also help to identify family relationships.

APPRENTICES, MASTERS AND FREEMEN

All over Britain, street names such as Cornmarket, Fisher's Row and Brewer's Lane stand as testament to the many trades and crafts practised by our forebears, many going back at least to the Middle Ages. The existence and usefulness of related records varies greatly, but where they do exist, they can be invaluable in updating your family tree.

Each trade or craft had a distinct hierarchy:

Apprentice From as young as ten years of age, children (mostly boys) could be apprenticed to a chosen trade – usually that of their father – for a period of seven years. An apprenticeship indenture was drawn up, and a fee paid by their parents (or, in the case of paupers, by the Overseer of the Poor – see page 101). Most apprentices lived with the master to whom they were apprenticed and would be clothed and fed at his expense.

Journeyman (from the French 'jour' for day, as they were paid a daily wage) – once out of their indentures, apprentices usually worked for a while with freemen (see below) to gain experience.

Freeman On successful completion of a test (known as a 'master piece'), apprentices and journeymen were 'freed' to set up their own shop or business, and to take on apprentices and journeymen of their own. Becoming a freeman also entitled them to vote, to be exempted from paying market and fair tolls and from being conscripted into the armed forces.

Master A fully qualified (and usually very experienced) freeman in charge of one or more apprentices.

Apprenticeship books

Official registers of apprentices began in 1710, when a stamp duty on indentures was introduced, and continued until 1811. The registers were compiled by Stamp Office clerks from information supplied by local duty collectors, and recorded the following information:

▶ Name, address and trade of the master to whom the child was apprenticed.
▶ Name of the apprentice.
▶ Dates of the apprenticeship.
▶ Up to 1752, the name and sometimes place of residence of the apprentice's father (sometimes the mother's name is included as well as, or instead of, that of the father).

Tips for searching apprenticeship books

▶ Entries are arranged by collection area, so from 1774 onwards you need to know the town, city or parish in which your ancestor was apprenticed, and this should also give you a rough idea of where the duty would have been paid.
▶ Pauper apprentices were funded by charities or their local parish and were therefore exempt from Stamp Duty, so they won't appear in these registers (see the Poor Law Records on pages 100–2).
▶ Separate registers were kept for apprentices in the home counties and for those apprenticed to London livery companies, so you will need to consult London archives for these (see page 121).

Where to find records

The National Archives holds Apprenticeship Books from 1710 to 1811, which can be downloaded as a PDF free of charge.

❶ It is useful to locate the records through the relevant Research Guide for Apprentices, as this gives helpful guidelines. Go to **www. nationalarchives.gov.uk**, click **The Catalogue** and then **Research Guides**

❷ From here, select **Apprenticeship records**, then on the next screen scroll down to 'Apprenticeship Books, 1710–1811'.

DID YOU KNOW?

Apprentices were often forbidden to marry until they had completed their indentures, so if you have been struggling to find details of an ancestor's marriage, discovering his apprenticeship records will at least suggest the earliest likely date for him to have tied the knot.

TRY THIS

Stamp duty on indentures was payable up to a year after the expiry of the indenture, so you might need to search through the records for several years to find the relevant entry.

occupations

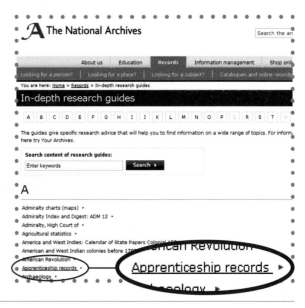

❸ In the 'Apprenticeship Books' section, click **DocumentsOnline**. This takes you to the main 'Digital Microfilm' section

---

3. Apprenticeship Books, 1710-1811

From 1710 to 1811 the Commissioners of Stamps kept registers of the money they received from the duty on indentures. These registers now form the Apprenticeship Books (IR 1) which can be viewed digitally through DocumentsOnline (see below for information on indexes to these records). Duty on indentures was payable by the master at the rate of 6d (sixpence) for every £1 under £50 which he received for taking on the apprentice, and the rate of 1s (one shilling) for every £1 above £50. The deadline for payment was one year after the expiry of the indenture. It might be necessary to search the records of several years' payments in order to find a particular entry, even when the date of the indenture is known.

TRY THIS

You may also find it useful to look at the sample entry, to give you an idea of how the records will look and what sort of information you can expect to gain from them.

❹ Click **What's available**, then scroll down to and click **Board of Stamps: Apprenticeship Books**. These are registers of payments received from the duty on indentures. Registers are listed chronologically, followed by indexes of masters. Note that 'City' refers to London, while 'Country' refers to other parts of the country

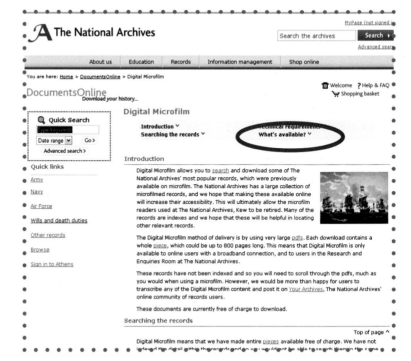

5 If there is a register that interests you, click **See Details**, then on the next screen click **Add to shopping**

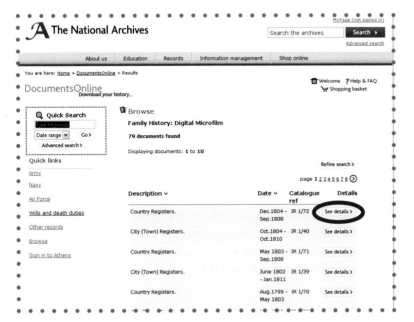

6 Click **Checkout**, then on the next screen enter your email address and click **Proceed with your download**. You will receive an email giving you a link to a page to download your document. Return to the 'Apprenticeship records' page (see Step 2), for information about other apprenticeship records held by The National Archives

The Society of Genealogists (www.sog.co.uk), which created the index at The National Archives, and the Guildhall Library (www.cityoflondon.gov.uk) also hold copies. The Guildhall Library gives details of relevant books, which you can reserve online, but you need to visit the library to view the books.

Local record offices may hold apprenticeship books and associated records.

Family history societies may have published details of local apprenticeships, so it is worth contacting the society covering your ancestor's region to see what they have.

Livery companies hold records relating to London's livery companies (see pages 122–3).

DID YOU KNOW?

Many apprenticeships, particularly before 1710, were informal agreements, and there may have been no signed papers. Any paperwork that did exist has almost certainly not survived.

TRADE GUILDS AND LIVERY COMPANIES

The forerunners of today's trade unions, the medieval trade guilds became known as livery companies due to the distinctive, brightly coloured 'livery' (or uniform) worn by senior members for official parades and functions. There were over 100 livery companies in the City of London, responsible for regulating the standard of goods, checking weights and measures and ensuring fair wages and working conditions for their members. Many were also involved in charitable works with a strong religious influence.

Most livery companies prefixed their names with 'The Worshipful' – as in The Worshipful Company of Blacksmiths – but a few are simply known as 'The Company of...', or 'The Guild of...'.

Although livery companies are normally associated with London, there were some livery companies in other towns and cities of the UK, and any surviving records will be held by the relevant county record office.

Trade Guild/livery company records

Many of the Trade Guilds and livery companies still exist, albeit in a very different form, and have their own archives. You can find out more about individual companies at the Livery Companies Database:

1 Go to **http://81.130.213.163:8002/cgi-bin/lcl.exe** and click on the company that interests you, say 'The Worshipful Company of Fishmongers'

2 A record for the Worshipful Company of Fishmongers will come up on the screen, with a link to their official website. Records held vary from one company to another, but they are worth investigating

Search the Guildhall Library online

The Guildhall Library (www.cityoflondon.gov.uk) holds records for the City of London livery companies, including apprenticeship and memberships records, company constitutions, details of property, and financial and charity records. A list of companies covered can be found at www.history.ac.uk/gh/livlist.htm:

1 Go to **www.history. ac.uk/gh/livlist.htm** and click on the company you are interested in, here 'Distillers'

2 On the resulting page and you will get details of the Guildhall's holdings relating to that company. You then need to visit the library to view the material

List of companies

Air Pilots and Air Navigators, Apothecaries, Armourers and Braziers

Bakers, Barbers (ca. 1540-1745 Barber Surgeons), Basketmakers, Blacksmiths, Bowyers, Brewers, Broderers, Brown Bakers, Butchers

Carmen, Carpenters, Clockmakers, Clothworkers, Coach and Coach Harness Makers, Combmakers, Cooks, Coopers, Cordwainers, Curriers, Cutlers

Distillers, Drapers, Dyers

Fanmakers, Farmers, Farriers, Fellowship Porters, Feltmakers, Fishmongers, Fletchers, Founders, Framework Knitters, Fruiterers

Gardeners, Girdlers, Glass Sellers, Glaziers, Glovers, Gold and Silver Wyre Drawers, Goldsmiths, Grocers, Gunmakers

Haberdashers, Horners

Innholders, Ironmongers

Joiners and Ceilers

Leathersellers, Longbowstringmakers, Loriners

Makers of Playing Cards, Masons, Mercers, Merchant Taylors, Musicians

Needlemakers

Records available

Records held by the Guildhall Library and some livery companies include the following registers and books:

Freemen Admission Registers list freemen alphabetically, and include name, address, date of admission, method of admission (such as by successful completion of an apprenticeship, patrimony, honour or redemption) and the fee paid.

Quarterage books record quarterly membership fees, and may include members' addresses, occupations and date membership ended (usually on the member's death). The disadvantage of these books is that they are not in alphabetical order.

Stamp Duty Freedom Registers recorded details of payments made to the Crown, and may include names and admission dates of freemen.

Court minutes and financial accounts may contain useful details about members, but can be time-consuming to search.

Poll books for the City of London list liverymen only, and may be arranged by company or alphabetically by individual.

▶ Occupations

LEGAL PROFESSIONS

If you had ancestors in the legal profession, they should be fairly easy to trace, as detailed records have been kept since 1775. As with trades and crafts, sons often followed their father into the profession, so you could discover a wealth of information about several members of your family.

Attorneys (known as solicitors since 1875) were generally responsible for conducting legal business on behalf of private clients, such as drawing up wills, property deeds and marriage licences, managing estates and collecting rents. From 1728 attorneys were required to serve a five-year apprenticeship as an articled clerk, and to swear an oath before being admitted to a court to practise.

Next step

See pages 147–8 for more information about searching university records.

Barristers were able to plead in court on behalf of clients and were generally better qualified than attorneys. Most went to university (until 1832, that would have been Oxford or Cambridge), and then trained at one of the Inns of Court in London – Lincoln's Inn, Gray's Inn, Middle Temple and Inner Temple. From 1853, they would have had to pass an examination.

Where to find records

The National Archives (www.nationalarchives.gov.uk) holds records relating to the Central Courts, the Courts of Common Pleas, King's Bench, Exchequer, Equity, Chancery and Bankruptcy, the Supreme Court of Judicature, the Palatinates of Lancaster, Durham and Chester, and the Proctors in the High Court of the Admiralty and the Prerogative Court of Canterbury. These include:

TIP

Many of these records are arranged by court, so it will save time if you know which court your ancestor was admitted to.

- ▶ Rolls of Attorneys, which are usually arranged alphabetically and in order of admission to the court.
- ▶ Certificate Books containing the certificates required for attorneys and solicitors to be able to practise, renewed annually.
- ▶ Registers of articles of clerkship – arranged chronologically.
- ▶ Attorneys' admission papers, books and rolls, oath rolls, registers of affidavits and some indexes.

It is worth consulting the in-depth research guide 'Lawyers: Attorneys and Solicitors' (www.nationalarchives.gov.uk/records/research-guide-listing.htm) for a detailed guide to their holdings and links to relevant National Archives documents, registers and indexes, as well as advice on research.

The Law Society (www.lawsociety.org.uk and click **Library Online** on the right-hand side of the home page) was established in 1828 and holds records relating to attorneys and solicitors dating back to 1790, including admission lists and registers of articles of clerkship.

The Guildhall Library in London (www.cityoflondon.gov.uk) holds copies of the Law List from 1787 to 1975, which covers solicitors and barristers. For details of lawyers practising before the start of the Law List, try the individual holdings of the Inns of Court (see below).

Inns of Court (London) The four main Inns of Court hold records relating to barristers who joined the Inn. These include:

▶ Admission Registers – two volumes covering 1420–1893. These include date of admission as well as, in some cases, age on admission, place of origin, father's name and date called to the bar. Sometimes other biographical details are included.
▶ Chapel Registers – it was not unusual for members to marry in the Inns chapels, to have their children baptised there and to be buried there. There are separate registers for baptisms (1716–1806), marriages (1695–1754) and burials (1695–1852).

▶ Black Books – six volumes, covering 1422–1965. These give details of all those called to the bar. Not all who entered the Inn were called to the bar (that is, became qualified lawyers), and it was common before the 20th century to enter one of the Inns of Court without ever being called to the bar.
▶ The holdings for Grays Inn also include pension books.

Search the Inns of Court archives
The archives of the four Inns of Court can be accessed at:
▶ www.innertemple.org.uk/archive/itad/index. asp
▶ www.lincolnsinn.org.uk/index.php/library/ information-on-past-members
▶ www.middletemple.org.uk/library
▶ www.graysinn.info.

Each archive website includes information on accessing the collections and how to contact the archivists. For example, to find the name of a relative who worked at the Inner Temple:

1 Go to **www.innertemple.org.uk/archive/itad/index.asp** and click **Searching the database**

TRY THIS

If you are unsure which Inn your ancestor was admitted to, you can enquire at any of the four Inns, and if necessary your enquiry will be forwarded to the correct Inn.

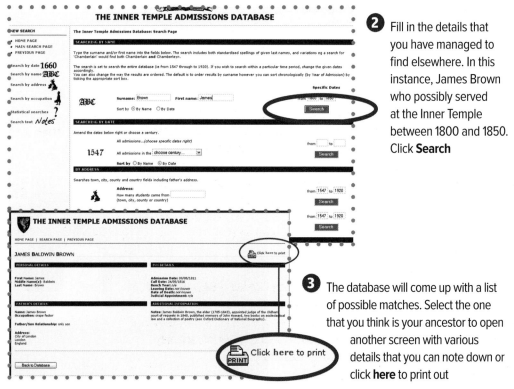

2 Fill in the details that you have managed to find elsewhere. In this instance, James Brown who possibly served at the Inner Temple between 1800 and 1850. Click **Search**

3 The database will come up with a list of possible matches. Select the one that you think is your ancestor to open another screen with various details that you can note down or click **here** to print out

MEDICAL PROFESSIONS

As with the legal profession, records for medical practitioners are fairly plentiful, in some cases going back as far as the 15th century. Unsurprisingly, records are particularly good from the 19th century, but there is a good chance you can trace your medical ancestors back further than that.

Surgeons and doctors

Early surgery was often practised by barbers as they had the necessary tools, and during the Middle Ages barbers and surgeons were part of the same livery company in London. It was not until 1745 that surgeons established their own identity by forming the Worshipful Company of Surgeons.

Surgical training was often through apprenticeship, but more formal training was introduced in Scotland in 1505, with the founding of the Royal College of Surgeons of Edinburgh, and in England in 1801 with the founding of the Royal College of Surgeons in London. Doctors also trained through apprenticeships, but by the 19th century they increasingly went to university to study.

Nurses and midwives

Before Florence Nightingale transformed the nursing profession, it was largely unregulated, with no training, and hospitals were often dirty and unhygienic. St Thomas's Hospital in London was the first to set up a training school for nurses in 1860, and State registration for nurses began as late as 1919.

Apothecaries

Originally traders of spices and herbs, apothecaries gradually expanded into the preparation and selling of drugs and medicines. In London, apothecaries were once part of The Worshipful Company of Grocers, but established The Worshipful Society of Apothecaries of London in 1617. In 1704 they won a landmark legal battle against the Royal College of Physicians to allow them to prescribe and dispense medicines, thereby becoming the forerunner of today's general practitioners. From 1815, apothecaries had to obtain a licence from the Society after completing a five-year apprenticeship.

Finding your medical ancestors

The best places to start are with the British Medical Directory (1845–date) and the Medical Register (1959–date), which give all kinds of useful biographical details about medical practitioners (including, from 1886, dentists). Copies are held by the Guildhall Library in London (www.cityoflondon.gov.uk), and may also be available in other regional record offices and libraries.

The Royal College of Surgeons in London (www.rcseng.ac.uk) has records going back to the mid-18th century relating mainly to Fellows of the College (those with FRCS after their names). The library is compiling biographies of past members, and those currently available can be found at http://livesonline. rcseng.ac.uk. You can also search the archive and museum catalogue at http://surgicat.rcseng.ac.uk, or make enquiries directly to the library.

Medical journals from hospitals and medical schools throughout the UK often include biographical information about their alumni, so if you know which hospital or school your ancestor trained at, it would be worth doing a quick online search to find the relevant journal.

County record offices will hold records relating to their local health authorities, so if you know which region your ancestor was practising in, this is definitely an avenue worth exploring. Before the mid-18th century, medical practitioners had to be issued with licenses by their diocesan bishop, and these are now usually held by CROs.

The Royal College of Surgeons of Edinburgh (www.rcsed.ac.uk) is a useful potential source for finding information about Scottish medical practitioners as it has archives dating back to the late 15th century. As in London, the incorporations of Surgeons and Barbers were joined until the 18th century, so some of the early records relate to barbers as well as surgeons. Holdings include college membership records, minute books, administrative records, letters, class cards and details of examinations, qualifications and honours. Some of the earliest records are in Old Scots and Latin.

The Royal College of Nursing Archives (http://rcnarchive.rcn.org.uk/) are worth visiting to track down nurses' records. Holdings include a chronological list of candidates, a printed register of members, members' files, registration fees, and details of deaths and registrations.

The National Archives (www.nationalarchives.gov.uk) also have records relating to nurses, including registers of paid nurses, details of appointments, a Hospital Records database, the Register of Nurses (1921–1975) and the Roll of Nurses (1945–1973).

The Worshipful Society of Apothecaries (www.apothecaries.org) holds apprenticeship bindings, membership records, candidates' qualification entry books, court minutes and registers of Licentiates if you have apothecary ancestors.

The Guildhall Library Manuscripts Section (www.history.ac.uk/gh/apoth.htm) also holds a large collection of records relating to apothecaries on microfilm, including freedom registers, apprentice bindings books, an alphabetical list of apprentices, quarterage books, court minutes, Licentiateship registers (with dates of qualification) and candidates' qualification entry books.

Search for a Fellow's obituary

The Royal College of Physicians holds the Munk's Roll, a collection of obituaries of past Fellows of the College dating back to 1518. They vary greatly in the amount of detail, from just a few lines to several paragraphs. Some don't even have dates, or dates are incomplete. Nevertheless, this is worth a look, as some of the records are very detailed and you can glean all kinds of information, including where they were educated and which hospital(s) they practised at, with relevant dates. You can either search or browse the indexes online. To search:

1 Go to **http://munksroll.rcplondon.ac.uk/** and click **Search**

2 In the resulting window, fill in the forename and surname details of the relative you are researching and click **Search** to reveal a list of possible matches. Click on the name that is of interest. The obituary appears in full

▶ Occupations

THE CLERGY

Clergymen generally qualified at university and were then appointed to a parish, which was usually the gift of a bishop or local patron. Alternatively, they could become chaplains for specific organisations (such as schools and universities), missionaries or preachers.

Many also held more than one living and would pay a curate to look after one parish while they were incumbent in another parish.

From 1792, all clergymen and preachers were required to be licensed by a bishop.

University records (see page 148) are a good place to start; their alumni lists will give useful biographical information, which will lead you to the relevant parish(es). Up to 1832 this would only have been Oxford or Cambridge, so this narrows down your search considerably.

The Institute of Historical Research has lists of bishops and higher clergymen going right back to 1066, as well as many other useful records relating to church history.

1 Go to **www.british-history.ac.uk** and click **Subjects**

2 Select **Ecclesiastical and religious history**, which will give you (among other records) lists of Higher Clergy of the Church of England, arranged chronologically. Select the one for the period you are interested in, say 1541–1857

3 You need to know where your ancestor practised, as records are arranged by diocese. So if you know your ancestor practised in the Bath and Wells diocese, for example, click **Bath and Wells diocese**

4 You now have a list of clergy and other church ministers arranged by positions held, so again it helps if you have some idea of whether your ancestor was a bishop or an archdeacon, for example

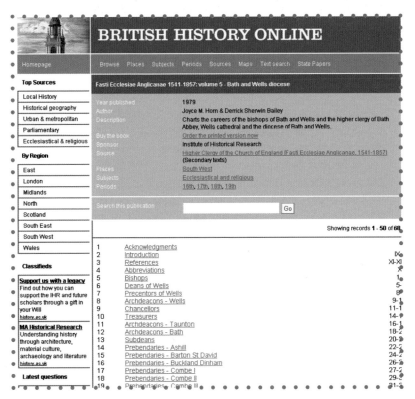

▶ Occupations

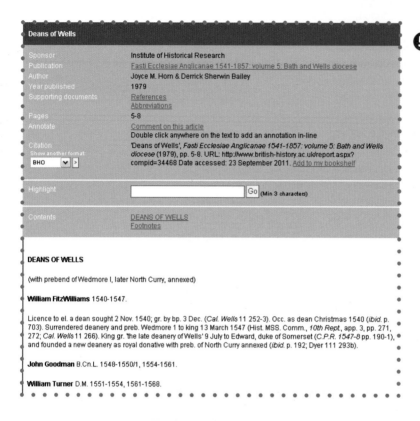

Deans of Wells

Sponsor	Institute of Historical Research
Publication	Fasti Ecclesiae Anglicanae 1541-1857: volume 5: Bath and Wells diocese
Author	Joyce M. Horn & Derrick Sherwin Bailey
Year published	1979
Supporting documents	References
	Abbreviations
Pages	5-8
Annotate	Comment on this article
	Double click anywhere on the text to add an annotation in-line
Citation	'Deans of Wells', *Fasti Ecclesiae Anglicanae 1541-1857: volume 5: Bath and Wells diocese* (1979), pp. 5-8. URL: http://www.british-history.ac.uk/report.aspx?compid=34468 Date accessed: 23 September 2011. Add to my bookshelf
Show another format:	
BHO ▼ ▶	

Highlight [   ] Go (Min 3 characters)

Contents   DEANS OF WELLS
           Footnotes

DEANS OF WELLS

(with prebend of Wedmore I, later North Curry, annexed)

William FitzWilliams 1540-1547.

Licence to el. a dean sought 2 Nov. 1540; gr. by bp. 3 Dec. (*Cal. Wells* 11 252-3). Occ. as dean Christmas 1540 (*ibid.* p. 703). Surrendered deanery and preb. Wedmore 1 to king 13 March 1547 (Hist. MSS. Comm., *10th Rept.*, app. 3, pp. 271, 272; *Cal. Wells* 11 266). King gr. the late deanery of Wells' 9 July to Edward, duke of Somerset (*C.P.R. 1547-8* pp. 190-1), and founded a new deanery as royal donative with preb. of North Curry annexed (*ibid.* p. 192; Dyer 111 293b).

John Goodman B.Cn.L. 1548-1550/1, 1554-1561.

William Turner D.M. 1551-1554, 1561-1568.

⑤ If you know that he was a Dean of Wells Cathedral, click **Deans of Wells** for a chronological list. The amount of detail varies from one person to another, but can include information such as dates of service, when presented to the deanery and by whom; when and why service was terminated; and sometimes dates of death

The Clergy List contains details of Anglican clergy from 1841 to 1858, including names, details of their livings, dates of appointments, how much each living was worth per annum and the name of the patron. Printed copies should be available in local studies centres and libraries. You can also search online at www.familyrelatives.com, but need to pay to view records.

Crockford's Clerical Directory was established in 1858, and gives much the same kinds of details as the Clergy List. Again, printed copies are usually available in local studies centres and libraries. There is an online version at www.crockford.org.uk, but again it is a subscription site, and only covers from 1968 onwards.

County record offices or diocesan offices may hold relevant records, including ordination papers, letters of recommendation, records from the local ecclesiastical courts and bishops' licences. If you know which county your ancestor practised in, you should find plenty of useful information here.

The Prerogative Court of Canterbury holds relevant wills (see page 96).

THE EMERGENCY SERVICES

If you had ancestors working in the emergency services, you should be able to track them down using the variety of resources available.

Policemen

Up to the 19th century, it was the responsibility of individual parishes to maintain law and order, for which they had local policemen and night watchmen. In London, where crime was considerably higher than in the provinces, Sir John Fielding (brother of author Henry Fielding) set up the Bow Street Runners in 1792, dividing London into seven police districts. The River Thames Police followed in 1798, and in 1805 the highways were patrolled by 'Robin Redbreasts' – armed police known for their distinctive red coats.

It was Sir Robert Peel's Metropolitan Police force – the famous 'bobbies' or 'peelers' – that came to be regarded as the first 'proper' police force when it was established in 1829. County police forces followed soon after and, by 1858, every county had its own police force.

Where to find records

The National Archives (www.nationalarchives.gov.uk) holds records for the London Metropolitan Police. These include:

▶ Staff records, of which the easiest to search are the alphabetical registers, but there is also a numerical register for searching by warrant number, as well as attestation ledgers, certificates of service and register of leavers. Most of these include name, rank, warrant number, division and dates of joining and leaving the service. The certificates of service also give the recruit's date of birth, trade, marital status, number of children, place of residence, and details of former employments. The register of leavers also includes comments on the officer's conduct.
▶ Pension records, which include physical description, date and place of birth, marital status and dates of service. Before 1923, The National Archive records also included names of the recruit's parents and next of kin (usually spouse).
▶ A nominal roll of officers of the Special Constabulary from 1875, giving service dates, place(s) of work and name of sponsors.
▶ Details of deaths in the line of duty, covering 1829–89.
▶ Details of promotions, dismissals and transferrals are included in the Police Orders (1829–1989).

Next step

More information can be found in The National Archives In-depth Research Guide to Police (www.nationalarchives.gov.uk/records/research-guides/transport-police.htm).

The Friends of the Metropolitan Police website (www.fomphc.org.uk) has useful information and links. The most useful is a listings of the first 3,247 officers, who joined between September 1829 and March 1830. These give their forename and surname, division served in, dates of service and reason for leaving, and are listed in warrant number order. If you don't know your ancestor's warrant number, you can search by surname by pressing **Ctrl+F** on your keyboard. To find this list:

1 Go to **www.fomphc.org.uk** and click **Family History**, then **Tracing Your Police Ancestors**

2 In the fourth paragraph, which talks about the officers with the first 3,247 warrant numbers, click where indicated

3 On the next screen, select one of the series of warrant numbers – for example, you might want the first 999 warrant numbers, relating to officers who joined the Force between September 1829 and February 1830

4 The list is arranged by warrant number, rather than alphabetically, so you might find it easiest to search for your ancestor by name by pressing **Ctrl+F** on your keyboard

5 There is also a chart showing the years in which warrant numbers were issued. This can be very useful for trying to determine an officer's warrant number if you have a rough idea of his date of joining. To find this chart, return to the 'Tracing your Police Ancestors' screen (as shown in Steps 1 and 2) and this time click where indicated in the third paragraph. The chart covers from 1829 to 2000

The Police Roll of Honour Trust (www.policememorial.org.uk) maintains rolls of honour for police officers who lost their lives in the line of duty from the 19th century to the present, covering all countries of the British Isles. Details vary, but all give the date of death and age at death, with a brief description of how death occurred, and details of any local memorials. If you know which county your ancestor served in, it is best to look at the regional rolls as they go back further. There is also a section giving details of national police memorials that you might like to visit. Click on the appropriate link in the Memorial menu.

The Metropolitan Police Historical Museum (www.met.police.uk/history/ crime_museum.htm) holds divisional records for 12 out of the 17 divisions in the Metropolitan Police, covering Westminster, Chelsea, Holborn, Kensington, King's Cross, Stepney, West Ham, Lambeth, Southwark, Islington, Greenwich and Holloway.

For regional police forces, records are most likely to be held by the relevant county record office, so that should be your first port of call. If they haven't got the records, they should be able to point you in the right direction.

The British Transport Police website (www.btp.police.uk/about_us/history.aspx) has a Roll of Honour, going back to 1858. Listings are by date and surname.

Firefighters
Early firefighters were employed by independent fire insurance companies, and their distinctive metal fire marks can still be seen on old buildings today. The UK's first municipal fire fighting force was established in Edinburgh in the 17th century and proved far more efficient. London followed suit in 1833, poaching Edinburgh's Chief Fire Officer, James Braidwood, and amalgamating ten independent companies to form the London Fire Engine Establishment (LFEE).

It was Braidwood who introduced a Brigade uniform and established the practice of recruiting fire fighters from the Royal Navy – a practice that persisted well into the 19th century. Nautical terms are still used in the Fire Brigade today.

Under Braidwood's successor, Captain Eyre Massey Shaw, the LFEE became the Metropolitan Fire Brigade, with its name changing again in 1904 to the London Fire Brigade.

◉ Occupations

With the passing of the Metropolitan Fire Brigade Act in 1865, provincial fire brigades began to form throughout England, Scotland and Wales, although the provision of fire brigades by local authorities didn't become a legal requirement until 1938. During the Second World War, many local authority fire brigades merged to form the National Fire Service, reverting to local authority control after the war.

The London Fire Brigade Museum (www.london-fire.gov.uk/Research.asp) is the best starting point for London firefighters. It has a large archive – not yet online, you need to visit the museum or use their enquiry service – covering the history of the Brigade up the start of the Second World War. Of most interest to the family historian is the collection of service records, which are a treasure trove of information, including:

▶ Full name.
▶ Date and place of birth.
▶ Education.
▶ Previous occupation(s).
▶ Marital status.
▶ Date of appointment.
▶ Promotions.
▶ Exams passed.
▶ Service medals awarded.
▶ Conduct (including 'offences' and the punishments given).
▶ Which fire station(s) the employee served at.

There are also log books, council minutes and information relating to specific fires. Access to the archives is by appointment only, but staff are happy to deal with enquiries.

For details of London firefighters from the Second World War onwards, contact the London Fire and Emergency Planning Authority by emailing the library at services@london-fire.gov.uk.

For all other fire fighters, you need to know the place of service and then contact the relevant county record office.

THE ARMED FORCES

To trace your ancestor through military records, it is helpful if you know which service he was in, his rank, regiment/ship/unit and dates of service. This will make it much easier to locate relevant documents if you are visiting archives in person, or speed up the process if you are searching online.

As well as giving you details of your ancestor's military career, service records and other related papers can confirm other essential details. These include dates of birth and death, place of birth, next of kin, education, marital status and much more.

The National Archives

The National Archives is the main repository for service records and other related papers for England and Wales, going back to the 16th century, so this should be your first port of call. You might find it helpful to start by reading their in-depth research guide to the armed forces at www.nationalarchives. gov.uk/records/research-guides/armed-forces.htm, which will give you an idea of the scope of their holdings and some tips on searching, as well as links to other repositories.

The National Archives holds millions of documents relating to the armed services, going back to the 18th century. Holdings include:

The Army (series reference WO): Army Lists giving details of officers' service dates, officers' birth certificates and other records, registers of baptisms and marriages in the British and Palestine Garrisons, First World War records (including records of Emergency Reserve officers, temporary commissions, Territorial Army officers, Women's Army Auxiliary Corps and Nursing service records), Second World War records (including rolls of honour and records relating to Prisoners of War) and Medal and Award rolls.

The Royal Navy (series reference ADM): Officers' service and pension records, officers' operational records, confidential reports, ships' muster rolls, certificates of service, registers of seamen's services, seamen's wills, records of medals, Victoria Cross registers, recommendations for honours and awards, ships' logs and journals, records of the Royal Naval Air Service (RNAS) and the Royal Naval Volunteer Reserves (RNVR), Royal Marines service records and records of the Women's Royal Naval Service (WRNS).

The Royal Air Force (series reference AIR): The Air Force List giving details of officers' careers from 1918, officers' service records, air combat reports,

REMEMBER
The National Archives collection is explained together with notes on using series references on pages 108–14.

DID YOU KNOW?
A large number of records relating to both world wars were destroyed by Second World War bombing, but many survived, so it is still worth checking if you think your ancestor served during this period.

service records of the Women's Royal Air Force (WRAF), recommendations for honours and awards, campaign medal index cards, operation books, crashes and casualties, Prisoner of War records and details of courts martial.

Other holdings for the armed services

The Society of Genealogists (www.sog.org.uk) holds copies of some of The National Archives records, including the Army Lists.

The Ministry of Defence holds recent service records, obtainable for a fee from MOD CS(RM)2, Bourne Avenue, Hayes, Middlesex UB3 1RF.

The National Army Museum (www.nam.ac.uk) has lots of information about the British Army, as well as useful records in its Temper Study Centre. These include the Army Lists, periodicals, memoirs, casualty lists and regimental and campaign histories. The website has helpful tips for family research, as well as a downloadable leaflet in PDF format.

The Imperial War Museum (www.iwm.org.uk) holds records relating to service personnel, including Rolls of Honour, Gallantry Awards and Commissions, personal papers (diaries and letters), journals, photographs and sound recordings.

The Royal Navy Museum (www.royalnavy.mod.uk) has a history of the service, and links to Royal Navy museums.

The Royal Air Force Museum (www.rafmuseum.org.uk) has its own library, with books, periodicals, maps and other ephemera relating to the RAF, as well as its own archive containing personal papers, aircrew logbooks, First World War casualty cards, records of accidents, company papers and Air Transport Auxiliary records. Both are searchable online, but give only listings – scanned documents are not available.

The National Records of Scotland (www.nas.gov.uk) have records for Scottish military ancestors. Try, too, www.scotlandspeople.com.

The National War Museum of Scotland (www.nms.ac.uk/our_museums/war_museum.aspx) holds regimental order books and papers, records of local militia and privates' diaries and papers.

The National Library of Wales (www.llgc.org.uk) is the place to go for Welsh military ancestors.

TIP

The earliest army records, dating back to the late 17th century, generally only mention officers. You are unlikely to find other ranks mentioned until the mid-18th century.

The Commonwealth War Graves Commission (www.cwgc.org) has records for tracing military ancestors' memorials.

There are also extensive records relating to the armed services on subscription sites such as www.ancestry.co.uk and www.findmypast.co.uk.

Search for a regimental museum

If you know which regiment your ancestor served, you could see whether there is a relevant regimental museum, as many such museums have their own archives. The Army Museums Ogilby Trust has a very useful 'Museum Search' page, where you can search by collection, regiment or region:

1 Go to **www.armymuseums.org.uk/ancestor.htm** and click the **Museum Search** tab

2 You can then search for your museum by collection, regiment or region. In this case, it's the King's Royal Hussars regiment. Click on the appropriate regiment in the drop-down box and then click **Go**

3 A choice of collections is given. Click on whichever link is the most appropriate, in this example, 'The Museum of The King's Royal Hussars' in Winchester. Full details of the contents of the museum are provided together with contact details, admission charges and other relevant information

OTHER OCCUPATIONS

The occupations detailed here are, of course, only a selection of some of the main areas of employment. There are many more trades and professions that your ancestors might have belonged to, some now obsolete. Servants, governesses, farmers, labourers, miners, railway and canal workers, fishermen and other marine trades, post office workers and businessmen are just a few of the other occupations you may come across.

Use directories

Published lists of people's names and trades began as far back as the 17th century and were originally mainly used to list merchants. They gradually expanded to include a wide variety of occupations, including merchants, tradesmen, craftsmen, the clergy, lawyers, medical practitioners and farmers. Most were published annually and covered specific areas of the country.

BE CAREFUL

Directories were often published a year after the information was collected, which means it could already be out of date by the time it came into print.

The best-known and most useful are Kelly's Directory, Pigot & Co and Bartholomew's Gazetteer, but some local firms produced their own directories as well. From the mid-19th century, listings were often by surname, trade, street or household.

Kelly's Directory was published by county and gives historical information on the county together with lists of Hundreds, Poor Law Unions and County Court districts, as well as an alphabetical listing of all the county's main towns and cities. Within that alphabetical listing are details of local businesses, trades people, landowners and charities, and all with postal addresses.

Pigot & Co was also a county guide, with a description of the county and lists of its major towns and cities, together with listings of local gentry, clergy and tradespeople. It is not as detailed as Kelly's, but still worth a look.

Bartholomew's Touring Atlas and Gazetteer of the British Isles was published primarily as a guide to Britain's roads, with a detailed index of towns and cities, but it also includes advertisements for local businesses and traders, so might be of some use.

You can usually find trade directories in local studies centres, libraries and county record offices or online at www.historicaldirectories.org, where you can search by location, decade or keyword, and download relevant pages free of charge. The Society of Genealogists (www.sog.co.uk) also holds copies of directories.

Use websites

A huge number of websites give useful links to a range of occupations. Some of the best include:

www.genuki.com/search Enter 'Occupations' in the search box and over 2000 results come up, many of them relating to specific regions of the British Isles. Alternatively, if you know where your ancestor lived and/or worked, you can look up 'Occupations' on the relevant county page.

www.rmhh.co.uk/occup/ has a useful and fascinating index of occupations, many of them virtually unheard of these days, or called by different names. Did you know, for instance, that a Gaffman is an old word for Bailiff? Warning: it's easy to get distracted on this site!

www.scotsfamily.com/occupations.htm is a similar site listing old Scottish occupations.

www.fhswales.org.uk/censuses/Occupations.htm is a list of old Welsh occupations.

DELVING FURTHER

By reading and following all the steps in this chapter, you will find out how to:

▶ **Delve deeper into your ancestors' lives by looking at school, university and hospital records**

▶ **Establish if you have any criminal ancestors**

▶ **Explore any potential royal or aristocratic ancestry**

SCHOOLS

Mass education is a relatively recent phenomenon; until the Education Act of 1870 (1872 in Scotland), only the rich could afford to send their children to schools. Poor children were often taught at home by their mothers or attended a charitable school, where there was as much emphasis on preparing them for a specific trade as on the Three Rs. Sunday Schools were also a popular choice for poorer children.

The 19th century saw the rise of Dame schools, which charged a very low fee and so were accessible to a greater number of children. Ragged schools for orphans and the very poor began in 1810, while correctional schools for delinquents began in 1857. Denominational schools were begun in 1833 and introduced the idea of pupil teachers (that is, pupils who were apprenticed to teach younger pupils while continuing with their own education).

After the passing of the Education Act, it became the responsibility of local authorities to provide compulsory education for children. Even then, some schools charged fees, and it was not until 1902 that free education was widely available to all children of 12 years and under.

The school-leaving age was raised to 15 in 1947, and to 16 in 1974. The 11 Plus examination was introduced in 1944, with the result determining whether a child was sent to a grammar school or secondary modern. This system continued until the introduction of comprehensive education in the early 1970s.

What school records can tell you
▶ Date of birth and/or age.
▶ Father's name.
▶ Place of residence.
▶ Dates of attendance.
▶ Details of achievements, any special awards, exam/test results.
▶ Conduct.
▶ An indication of the family's wealth at a given period.
▶ Names of other family members (siblings almost invariably attended the same schools, and sometimes you will find several generations at the same school).

Records available
The records that are available will vary from one repository to another, but generally you can expect to find:

▶ Attendance and admissions registers.
▶ Head teachers' log books, which recorded daily life at the school, including comments on attendance, lessons and conduct.
▶ Records and reports of sporting activities and other school events.
▶ Prize-giving lists.
▶ Financial records.
▶ Governors' minutes.
▶ Photographs.
▶ Private papers, such as letters, exercise books.
▶ School inspection reports.

▶ Delving Further

Find school records

1 Most schools have either retained their own records or deposited them with the local county record office. If you know which school your ancestor attended, enter the name of the school into a search engine as a first step, and this should give you a link to the official website

2 If there are no archives on a school's website, it is likely that they are with the county records office. One way to find the local county records office is to go to **www.genuki.org.uk** and select the relevant county page. This should give links to local repositories

3 Another option is to go to **www.genuki.org.uk/search** and enter the word 'schools' or 'education' into the search box. Click **Search** and a huge variety of resources are listed. Scroll through them to see if any are relevant to your research and click on the appropriate link

4 You might find your ancestor's school listed in a relevant Directory (see page 141)

5 The Society of Genealogists (www.sog.org.uk/library/intro.shtml) holds a large collection of school records, mostly from public schools, which includes full biographical details. The collection is arranged alphabetically and while you can view a list of the Society of Genealogists library holdings online, you need to visit the society to see the records

UNIVERSITIES

Until the 19th century, Oxford and Cambridge were the only two universities in England and Wales. Durham was founded in 1832, and from the mid-19th century, universities and other higher-education establishments spread rapidly throughout the British Isles. Scotland's earliest universities are Aberdeen, St Andrew's, Edinburgh and Glasgow, while Ireland's oldest university is Trinity College, Dublin.

What university records can tell you
▶ Dates of matriculation (entering the university) and graduation.
▶ Date of birth and/or age at matriculation.
▶ Place of residence at time of matriculation.
▶ Date left (if before graduation).
▶ Details of examination results.
▶ Extra-curricular activities, such as rowing or playing other sports for the university.
▶ Career details after leaving university.

▶ Delving Further

Records available

▶ Undergraduate admissions records.
▶ University registry.
▶ Examination records.
▶ Records of committees and other bodies.
▶ Administrative and financial records.
▶ Records relating to specific faculties of the university.
▶ Alumni lists and biographies.

How to find university archives

Universities are more likely than schools to retain their own records, so if you know which university your ancestor attended, your best starting point is to find that university online and see what its website says about archives. Most are happy to answer enquires.

As with schools, it is worth searching for universities on www.genuki.org.uk, which will produce a list of links to all sorts of useful websites (see page 142).

The Society of Genealogists (www.sog.org.uk/library) holds registers from the universities of Oxford, Cambridge, Aberdeen, Edinburgh, Glasgow, St Andrews and Dublin. You need to visit the library to see their records.

HEALING THE SICK

If you discover that one of your ancestors spent time in a hospital, the records described may add more details. Early hospitals were run by religious organisations, but after the Dissolution of the Monasteries responsibility for looking after the sick fell to local parishes. The foundation of hospitals relied on charitable donations, and they were often established on the same site as the dreaded workhouses, so there was often little distinction between the poor and the sick. It was not until the beginning of the 18th century that dedicated hospitals were established in London, principally as teaching hospitals and for caring for pregnant women. Other cities in the UK soon followed.

During the 18th century the wealthy could attend subscription hospitals, funded by public subscriptions and private donations, but sometimes the poor were admitted at the discretion of hospital staff (usually if they had an 'interesting' medical condition!). Specialist, private and isolation hospitals began to emerge during the 19th century, along with sanatoriums and convalescent and nursing homes.

How to find hospital records

Many hospital records have been deposited in local archives, so if you know which hospital – or even just which county – your ancestor was in, start by searching for the relevant county record office or Health Authority online. In some counties, the local Health Authority has retained its own archives, while others have amalgamated with the county record office.

The National Archives (www.nationalarchives.gov.uk) holds records of the Ministry of Health (later the Department of Health and Social Security) and other related organisations, including the Lunacy Commission, Board of Control and Special Hospitals, the General Nursing Council for England and Wales, the Medical Practices Committee and the Central Health Services Council and Central Council for Health Education (series reference MH).

REMEMBER

The National Archives collection is explained together with notes on using series references on pages 108–14.

The Hospitals Database is a joint project by The National Archives and the Wellcome Library. You can search by hospital or town, or both if you know them. A successful search will tell you:

▶ Current full name and address of the hospital plus previous names (if any).
▶ Year of foundation.
▶ Status (private or NHS) – some hospitals will have gone from private to NHS during the course of their lives – and type (e.g. mental health).
▶ What records are available, and where they can be found.

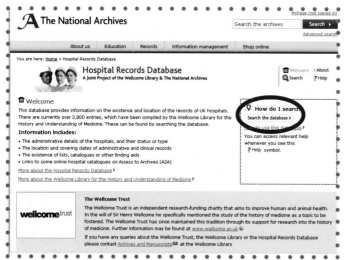

Use the Hospitals Database

1 Go to **www. nationalarchives.gov.uk/ hospitalrecords** and click **Search the database**

2 On the next screen, enter the name of the hospital you are searching for, and/ or the relevant town or city – for example, the Warneford Hospital in Oxford – and click **Search the database**

3 A list of search results comes up. In this example, there is just the one result – click **Details** for more information

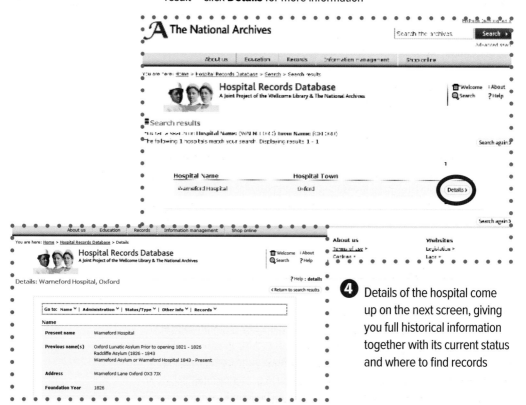

4 Details of the hospital come up on the next screen, giving you full historical information together with its current status and where to find records

CRIMINAL ANCESTORS

It was not until the 16th century that prisons began to be regarded as places of correction and punishment; before that, they were little more than holding centres for people awaiting trial. Those convicted of crimes were likely to be flogged, transported or executed, so even after the 16th century prisons were little used. Prison sentences didn't become commonplace until the 19th century.

Find prison records

If you know where your ancestor was tried and imprisoned, start at the relevant county record office where a range of useful records may include:

Prison registers usually give the prisoner's name, age, place of birth, physical description and, in later records, a photograph.

Gaolers' Journals include names of prisoners, dates of admission and discharge, and details of the crime for which they were imprisoned.

Quarter Session records normally dealt with minor crimes, and include records of court sittings, indictments detailing criminal charges, lists of prisoners and jurors, sworn statements and rolls of 'orders' detailing decisions made by JPs.

The National Archives (www.nationalarchives.gov.uk) has an extensive collection of criminal records, including:

▶ Annual criminal registers from 1805 to 1892, which give the prisoner's name, date and place of the trial, details of the verdict and the punishment.
▶ Calendars of prisons and prison registers from 1770 to 1949 – useful if you know which prison your ancestor was in.
▶ Court records from the Central Criminal Court (series ref. CRIM), Chancery (C), King's Bench (KB), Common Pleas (CP), Assize (ASSI) and the Supreme Court of Judicature (J).
▶ Prison records from the King's Bench, Fleet and Marshalsea Prisons (PRIS).
▶ Register of deaths in prison from 1914 to 1951 (PCOM 2/472).

In the 'Documents Online' section of the website (www.nationalarchives. gov.uk/documentsonline), you can access and download photographs and case details of inmates at Wandsworth Prison 1872–73. Each entry gives a photograph and detailed description of the prisoner, together with their date and place of birth, crime, sentence, place of conviction, release date, place of residence before the crime and intended residence after release.

DID YOU KNOW?

Unfortunates such as bankrupts, tramps and unmarried pregnant women were regarded as 'criminals', while Catholics were also persecuted, so if your ancestors fall into any of these categories you might find them mentioned in prison and court records.

▶ Delving Further

For more information about The National Archives' prison and court holdings, read the 'In-depth Research Guide' on 18th-, 19th- and 20th-century criminals at www.nationalarchives.gov.uk/records/research-guide-listing.htm.

The Society of Genealogists (www.sog.org.uk) holds Bernau's Index, an alphabetical listing of court depositions and proceedings from the Courts of Chancery and Exchequer.

The National Records for Scotland (www.nas.gov.uk) is the place to go for researching Scottish criminal ancestry.

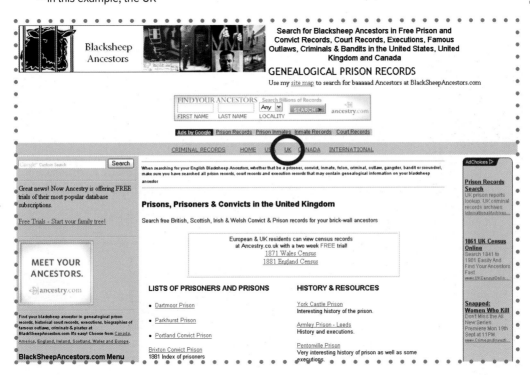

Search for your criminal ancestor online

If you don't know where your ancestor was imprisoned, a good place to start is the website Black Sheep Ancestors, where you can search by name for ancestors in the UK, USA and Canada free of charge. The website covers civil and criminal cases, so whether your ancestor was a hardened criminal or an occasional poacher, you might well find him/her here.

1 Go to **www.blacksheepancestors.com** and select the desired location – in this example, the UK

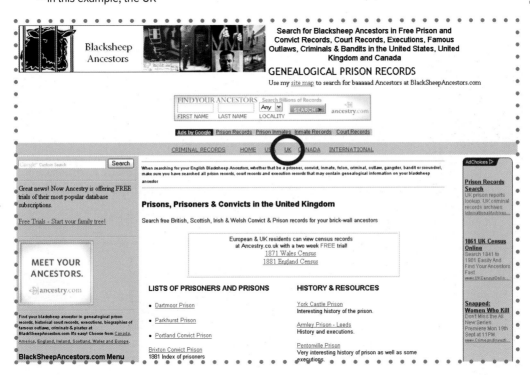

2 Click **Prison & Convicts Search**. This gives you a list of prisons in the UK, each with various lists of prisoners. If you have a rough idea of which prison your ancestor might have been in, and the possible dates of his incarceration, you can search the lists as described in the following steps

⏵ Delving Further

TRY THIS

If you only know your ancestor's place of birth, bear in mind that he/she might have moved away at some point, so won't necessarily have been sent to the prison nearest to his/her birth town. So if you don't find your ancestor in what seems the most obvious prison, try searching further afield.

3 For example, if you suspect your ancestor, John Fennel, was in Dartmoor Prison in the 1870s, click **Dartmoor Prison**

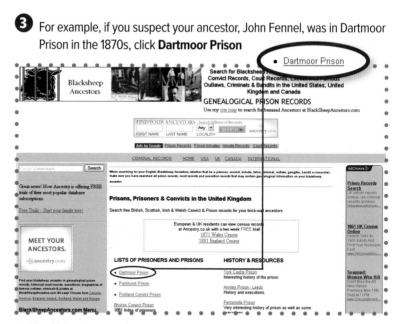

4 Then click **Surnames A – K** to bring up an alphabetical list of prisoners in 1871

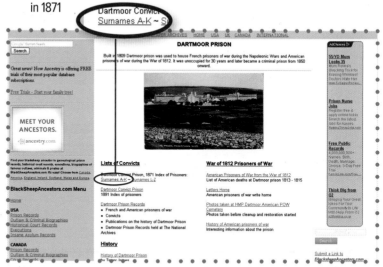

5 Press **Ctrl+F** on your keyboard, and type 'Fennel' in the dialog box that opens. Click **Next**. If your ancestor is listed, he will be highlighted in the text. Check the date of birth and place of birth against your other sources to see if this was indeed your ancestor

If you draw a blank using the name search on Black Sheep Ancestors, or get an unwieldy list of results, you could try some of the other searches on this site, which includes:

▶ **Outlaw and Criminal Ancestor Search** contains biographies of famous and not-so-famous criminals, so you might find something useful here.
▶ **Court Records** links to details of criminal proceedings at the Old Bailey, London, from 1674 to 1834.

▶ You can also link to a list of wills and bequests from Liverpool and Merseyside.

▶ **Executions** has several searchable lists of executions in the British Isles – worth a look if you know or think your ancestor met his end at the hands of the hangman.

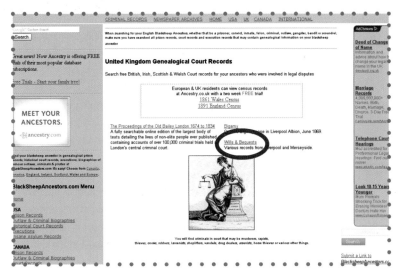

▶ Delving Further

TRANSPORTATION

Transportation of criminals was popular from about the 16th to the 19th centuries and had the dual advantage of ridding society of criminals and populating the various British colonies gradually being established around the world. So if you are looking for criminal ancestors, you might well need to look overseas.

North America and the West Indies were the usual destinations for criminals during the 16th and 17th centuries, but the War of Independence in America in the late 18th century, and the increased use of slaves by plantation owners in the West Indies, meant these were no longer viable options. From 1787 until transportation finished in 1868, Australia was the main destination.

Where to find transportation records

The National Archives where the holdings are mainly in the series reference HO (indicating that they were records held by the Home Office, see page 112), and include:

- ▶ Registers of transported convicts.
- ▶ Lists of convicts sent to New South Wales, Tasmania and Bermuda.
- ▶ Doctors' medical logs on convict ships.
- ▶ Petitions from convicts and their families before and after transportation.
- ▶ Lists of crew and prisoners on convict hulks.
- ▶ Assizes at which an agreement was drawn up for a ship to transport convicted criminals; records usually include the name of the ship and its destination.

The National Archives' In-Depth Research Guide, The Transportation of Convicts, gives detailed information and relevant links (www.nationalarchives. gov.uk/records/research-guide-listing.htm).

County record offices may also hold details of court sessions at which the convict was tried and sentenced to transportation. This is a useful option if you know where your ancestor lived at the time of his/her crime.

Search for records online

The British Convict Transportation Registers 1787–1867 database (www.slq. qld.gov.au/info/fh/convicts) is a useful online resource, compiled from Home Office records. This is not an exhaustive collection, but the vast majority of the estimated 160,000 convicts transported to Australia are included here.

1 Go to **www.slq.qld.gov.au/info/fh/convicts** and enter the name of your relative in the 'Find a convict' box. Click **Go**. You can also search by the name of the convict, name of the ship or year of arrival. As always, the more search factors you know, the quicker and more fruitful your search will be

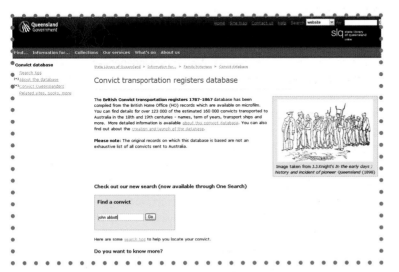

2 A list of results appears. Scroll through them and select any that you think are relevant to your researches

3 From the list of results, click **Details** on a selected entry to find out more about that convict. Information from a successful search includes:

▶ Name of ship.
▶ Number of convicts on the ship.
▶ Date of transportation.
▶ Destination.
▶ Where trial took place.
▶ Length of sentence.
▶ Location of original record.

▶ Delving Further

IMMIGRATION

Britain has always been a melting pot of nationalities; from ancient times, Romans, Saxons, Vikings and Normans have left their mark on our ancestry, and there are few today who don't have forebears from one of these nations. In the 16th century, Flemish ('Walloons') and French ('Huguenots') Protestants fled to our shores to escape persecution from the Catholics in their own countries, while other European races subsequently added to the mix from the 17th century onwards.

TRY THIS

It can be difficult to identify black ancestors before the 19th century, as they were often given English names by their masters, and their place of origin not always recorded. If you are struggling to trace the origins of an ancestor, it is possible that he/she was a black immigrant.

Black immigration – often thought of as a 20th-century phenomenon – actually dates back to at least the 16th century, with many coming over initially as slaves or servants. By the 18th century Britain had a substantial black population. The chance of a white person today having at least one black ancestor is surprisingly high.

Jargon buster ▶

Naturalisation
A naturalised person is permanently resident in another country and has been given citizenship.

From the 20th century, immigration from African nations, the Caribbean, China, India and Pakistan has added considerably to the gene pool, especially as inter-racial marriages become increasingly common.

How to trace immigrant ancestry

The National Archives holds a range of documents relating to immigrants, going right back to the 13th century. Of these, the most useful are:

- ▶ Certificates of alien arrivals (series reference HO2), which are arranged by arrival port and include the following information: nationality, profession, date of arrival, last country visited, signature.
- ▶ Indexes to denization and naturalisation, which should give the country of origin, as well as other useful details.
- ▶ Returns of strangers living in London and other towns and cities. Before the Act of Union of 1707, this would have included the Scots and Irish.
- ▶ Non-parochial registers from non-British churches in London and other towns and cities, including details of births, baptisms, marriages and burials, from the 16th to the 20th centuries.
- ▶ Embarkation lists and Passenger lists showing name of aliens, date and port of arrival and country of origin.

Census returns (see pages 26–46) should give useful details about immigrant ancestors; once you know the date of arrival, you can search the next available census return.

Marriage certificates of immigrants (again, searchable once you know dates of arrival) should give the names and occupations of the parents, who may still be in the country of origin.

There is also a comprehensive range of immigration records on www.ancestry.co.uk. These include passenger arrival records, naturalisation records, border crossings, emigration records, passports, and convict transportation records (see also pages 156–7). You can search the online database for free, but will have to pay to see the records:

1 Go to **www.ancestry.co.uk**. Click **Search**, then **Immigration & Travel**

2 Enter as many details as you can in the boxes. To narrow down your search to various categories, such as 'Passenger Lists', 'Citizenship & Naturalisation Records' or 'Immigration & Emigration Books', click your chosen category on the list on the right. Click **Search**

3 You will then be shown a list of possible results. Click **View Image** to see the record

Jargon buster

Denization
A denizen is a person who is permanently resident in another country but enjoys only certain rights of citizenship.

BE CAREFUL

Don't assume that the name of the last country visited is the country of origin; immigrants often made their voyage here in stages, especially if they were coming from far away.

▶ Delving Further

EMIGRATION

People have left these shores for a variety of reasons; to escape economic hardship or religious persecution or to settle in new overseas colonies. There have been periods of intense emigration; the Irish potato famine of 1845–47, for example, saw many Irish fleeing to America or England, while the notorious Highland Clearances of the 18th and 19th centuries saw many impoverished Scots forcibly moved abroad.

Records of people leaving the country are much less plentiful than those for people arriving, so generally you will have to look to the country your ancestors moved to for records.

Find emigrant ancestors

The National Archives has records relating mainly to emigrants who left Britain on government business, and child emigration, including the emigration of pauper children to ease the pressure on the Poor Law Unions. Holdings at The National Archives include:

▶ Passenger lists giving the names of people leaving ports in England, Wales, Scotland and Ireland between 1890 and 1960 for destinations outside Europe.
▶ Colonial Office records detailing those who emigrated to North American colonies that later became Canada.
▶ Treasury records relating to people who had already emigrated to the colonies or were planning to do so.
▶ Microfilm copies of the archives of the Hudson's Bay Company, founded in Canada in 1670.
▶ Various records relating to emigration to Australia and New Zealand, including registers of passengers, correspondence and entry books.
▶ Records relating to the emigration of pauper children between 1850 and 1909.

The Society of Genealogists (www.sog.org.uk) has collections relating to America, Canada, Australia, New Zealand, India and the West Indies, which might yield some useful information.

TRY THIS

Find out as much as you can about your ancestor from his/her country of settlement first; this will make it easier to trace your ancestor's origins in Britain. For example, your relative may have emigrated to the United States early in the 20th century, in which case a starting point might be the passenger lists on the Ellis Island website: www.ellisisland.org/search/passSearch.asp

Search online using www.ancestorsonboard.com

The website www.ancestorsonboard.com is probably the most useful website for searching emigrant passenger lists, and covers the period 1890 to 1960.

1 Go to **www.ancestorsonboard.com**

2 Enter as many known details as you can to narrow down your search as much as possible. Click **Search**

3 The search results will give you exact matches as well as details of records that almost match your criteria. You have to pay to view transcripts, but can get useful extra details just from the search. In this example, which gives four possible exact matches, we now have the year of birth, year of departure and departure port

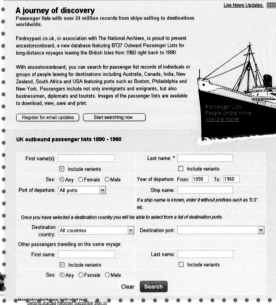

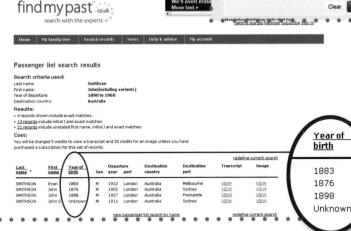

4 With these extra details, you can now either add information into your family tree (for example, you might not have known the year of birth up to this point), or use the details from research already carried out to identify which of those listed is your ancestor

Another useful website to try is The Ships List (www.theshipslist.com), which does much the same thing.

'MISSING' BIRTHS

If you are struggling to find your ancestor in the births registers, it could be that he/she was orphaned or adopted.

Orphans and foundlings

Orphans were much more common before the 20th century than they are now, because the adult life expectancy was so much lower. It was not unusual to lose both parents during childhood; it was also common for women to die during childbirth.

Sometimes orphans were taken in by other members of the family (see Adoption and fostering, page 164), but in many cases they became the responsibility of the authorities. Similarly, foundlings – children who had been abandoned, probably due to being illegitimate – came under the care of local authorities, which usually meant being sent to the workhouse.

Find records of orphans and foundlings

Few records of orphanages have survived, and the parentage of foundlings was rarely known. Some may have been baptised and therefore appear in the parish registers, but details will almost certainly be incomplete. Any dates given may not be accurate.

Dr Barnardo's homes for orphans and the very poor began in 1866, with the first home for boys being founded at Stepney, London, in 1870, and the first home for girls following three years later in Barkingside, Essex. The Barnardo's archive (www.barnardos.org.uk) holds photographs and comprehensive records relating to the children cared for by the charity, as well as a detailed online directory of all its former homes. If you think your ancestor may have been a Barnardo's child, the charity will undertake the necessary research for you, for a small fee.

Barnardo's children were given an education and taught a trade; many of the boys joined the Army or Royal Navy, while girls went into domestic service, so you may be able to find out more about their lives through occupational records (see pages 118–42).

Barnardo's was also involved with the Government's child migration policy of the 19th and early 20th centuries, which was intended to try and give poor children better opportunities overseas. Many were sent to Australia and Canada, so you might be able to trace them through emigration records (see pages 160–1).

The Foundling Hospital was established by Thomas Coram in 1747 to care for orphaned and abandoned children from all over the UK. Happily for family researchers, the hospital staff kept meticulous records, most of which are now held by the London Metropolitan Archives (www.cityoflondon.gov.uk/lma). These include admittance records, baptism registers, inspection books, petitions for admission, inspection books and children's billet books.

There is a very useful leaflet, downloadable from the website as a PDF, called Finding Your Foundling, which gives full details of the hospital's holdings. Go to the home page and search for 'Foundling Hospital'. Scroll down the page until you reach the leaflet.

The Foundling Museum (www.foundlingmuseum.org.uk) opened in 2004, and has many more objects and documents of interest on display, telling the story of the hospital and the lives of its foundlings. As with the Barnardo's children, foundlings were usually taught a trade or put into apprenticeships, and details of those apprenticeships are on display at the museum, which means you can follow your foundling ancestor's life beyond the hospital. Other items on display include the General Register for 1741–57, instructions left by the children's parents, an infirmary book detailing children's illnesses and relevant dates and tokens left by mothers in the hope of one day being

DID YOU KNOW?

Only adoptees can apply for original birth certificates, so unless your adopted ancestor is still alive and willing to do this, your trail could run cold at this point.

reunited with their children. Go to the website to find out more about the collections and the museum's opening times.

Adoption and fostering

Legal adoption didn't begin until 1927; before that, people could take in other people's children on a purely informal and unofficial basis and there were rarely any written agreements. Children were often given the surname of their adoptive parents, making their original parentage virtually impossible to trace.

Finding adoption and fostering records

The Adopted Children's Register was established in 1927, and is held by the General Register Office for England and Wales (www.gro.gov.uk/gro/content/adoptions), the General Register Office for Scotland (www.gro-scotland.gov.uk) and also the General Register Office for Northern Ireland (www.nidirect.gov.uk/gro).

Adoption certificates, also held by the General Register Office, are available as short certificates and full certificates. A short certificate tells you:

▶ Date of birth.
▶ Place and country of birth.
▶ Adoptive forename.
▶ Adoptive surname.
▶ Gender.

A full certificate also shows:

▶ Name and surname of adoptive parents.
▶ Address and occupations of adoptive parents.
▶ Date of adoption order.
▶ Date on which adoption was granted.
▶ Name of the court.

BLUE BLOOD

A surprising number of us might have royal or noble blood in our veins – sometimes by direct descendancy, but frequently through illegitimacy, as members of the Royal family and the aristocracy were famous in centuries past for their dalliances.

Trace royal or aristocratic lineage

If you think you might have royal or aristocratic ancestors, the best place to start is with Burke's Peerage, the standard reference guide to royalty, the nobility and landed gentry.

Copies of Burke's various publications – *Burke's Peerage and Baronetage*, *Burke's Landed Gentry*, *Burke's Extinct Peerage* and *Burke's Extinct Baronetage* – are available in most libraries and local studies centres, while the associated website (www.burkespeerage.com) is an ever- growing online archive.

1 Go to **www.burkespeerage.com** and enter your name (or any surname from your family tree) in 'Try a Free Family Search'

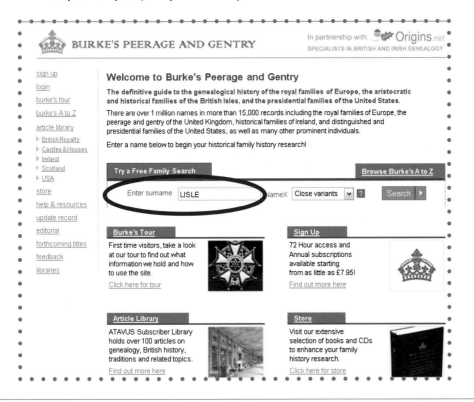

2 Click **Search** to produce a list of possible family connections

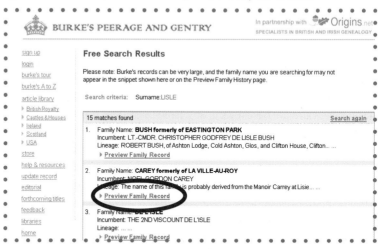

3 If any connections look promising, click **Preview Family Record** for further details of a person's name and title. To view the full record, you will need to sign up. Annual subscriptions are £64.95, but you can pay for 72-hour access for as little as £7.95

4 You can also browse through the 'A–Z directory' free of charge, although again you will need to sign up to view full records

5 Once you have a full record, you should then have sufficient details to continue searching the family line, as described elsewhere in this guide

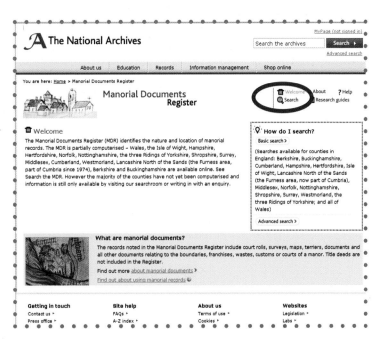
MANORIAL RECORDS

You may find that one of your ancestors was a Lord of the Manor – or he could have been one of the many manorial workers or tenants.

Dating from the 11th century, a manor was an agricultural estate used as a unit of local government in England and Wales. At its head was a lord of the manor, and it would be administered by a manorial court. Manors pre-date parishes, and so can help you trace your family back to before the era of parish registers. The system was abolished in 1922.

How manorial records can help with your family history

Tenancy changes (which usually occurred on the death of a tenant) are recorded in court rolls, court books and admittances, which give names of the deceased and of the incoming tenants, their relationship (tenancies were often passed through families) and relevant dates. Although dates given may be approximate, they can help to piece together your early family tree.

Call books and call lists also note deaths of tenants, but lists were often made some time after the event (sometimes years later), so dates are unreliable.

Details of individuals can be found among lists of jurors and manorial officials, and perhaps in records of crimes

Find manorial records

The National Archives Manorial Documents Register is the best starting point. This gives details of the locations of old manorial records. Parts of the Register are searchable online, by manor name, parish or county; all other parts of the register need to be viewed at Kew.

 Go to **www. nationalarchives. gov.uk/mdr** and click **Search**

2 Enter the name of the manor you are interested in – in this example, Aldworth in Berkshire – and click **Search**. A list of results comes up (in this example, just one). Click on the one that interests you

3 You will now see a list of records for that location, complete with references and the relevant repositories

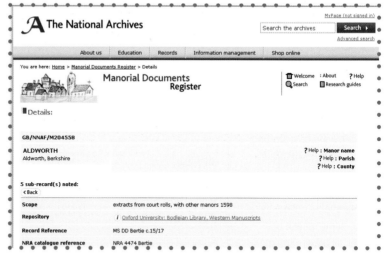

4 As you will see when you search the Kew records, many of the manorial records are held at The National Archives, by county record offices and private institutions such as universities. So once you've identified the location for the records you are interested in, your next step is to visit the relevant repository and glean as many facts from the records about your ancestor as you can. Although the records vary in their detail, you might be able to identify family relationships and find out at least approximate dates

OTHER USEFUL RECORDS

If you've drawn a blank among all the 'usual' sources of family history, there are lesser-known sources you can try.

Poll Books and Electoral Registers

Poll Books date from 1696, when ballots were far from secret, and published people's names together with details of how they voted. Information recorded in poll books included:

▶ Voter's full name.
▶ Place of residence.
▶ Occupation (not always included).
▶ Address of the property, or freehold, that entitled him to vote.

Voters Lists and Freeholders Registers provide similar information, while the annual Sheriff's Lists give details of all male freeholders in the country who could be called upon for jury service.

Electoral Registers were introduced in 1832 with the passing of the Reform Act and this annual list of everyone qualified to vote is still in use today. These are particularly useful for clarifying the length of time your ancestor lived at a particular address – which can also help determine the place of birth of any of his offspring.

Who could vote?

It is only relatively recently that entitlement to vote was widespread; up to the 19th century there were several restrictions on who could and could not vote. Key dates for entitlement to vote are:

▶ 1918: all men over the age of 20, plus some female property owners.
▶ 1928: all men and women over the age of 20.
▶ 1970: all men and women over the age of 18.

Where to find Poll Books and Electoral Registers

County record offices, other local archives and the Institute of Historical Research (www.british-history.ac.uk) hold Poll Books, Sheriff's Lists and Freeholders Registers

Local archives hold electoral registers and recent registers are searchable on www.192.com.

delving further

DID YOU KNOW?

Poll books are not necessarily a good way of discovering your ancestors' political allegiances, because tenants often voted the way their landlords wished them to for fear of being evicted. But you can glean other useful personal details about your ancestors from them.

▶ Delving Further

Taxes

Early tax records were surprisingly detailed, giving much the same information as the later censuses. Information contained in tax records included:

- ▶ Taxpayer's name.
- ▶ Place of residence.
- ▶ Details of the property.
- ▶ Details of family and servants living at the property.

There have been a variety of different taxes levied over the years, including Land Tax (1693–1963), Hearth Tax (1662–96), Window Tax (1696–1851) and Income Tax (1799).

The National Archives hold taxation records before 1689.

County record offices or local archives also keep taxation records among the Quarter Sessions reports.

NEWSPAPERS

Local and national newspapers can be a great source of family history. The main things likely to be of use are announcements of births, marriages and deaths, obituaries, court reports, coroner's reports, theatre/music reviews (if your ancestor was in showbiz, either as a professional or amateur) and other news items involving your ancestor.

The drawback with newspapers is that few have been indexed, so searching through them could be a very lengthy process, unless you have some idea of exactly what you are looking for and the approximate date.

The British Library Newspaper Collection (see page 72) is the best starting point, as it has a vast collection of national, regional and overseas newspapers, magazines and journals, most of which have been catalogued.

County record offices, local libraries and studies centres hold collections of local newspapers, and often one or two nationals (such as *The Times*) as well. They may be partially or completely catalogued.

BUILD YOUR TREE ON A PC

By reading and following all the steps
in this chapter, you will find out how to:

- **Create a family tree on your PC and online**

- **Add multimedia to your family tree**

- **Share your tree**

CHOICES OF SOFTWARE

Paper records are fine if you are happy to record your family history in this way, but the increasingly sophisticated software available can make your life very much easier and save you a lot of time.

Advantages of using software

► Easier to organise your data.
► No need to keep re-typing the same or similar information.
► Ready-made forms for you to enter your information into.
► You can add other media, such as photographs, images of documents, oral history recordings and video clips, to really bring each record to life.
► You can add as much or as little information as you like, from the most basic details to full biographies.
► You can share information more easily with other family members.
► You have an unlimited storage capacity.
► It is easy to add and update records, move from one record to another and quickly find a specific record.
► It clarifies where you still have gaps in your research.

Disadvantages of using software

► There is the possibility of losing everything if your computer crashes – so always keep original handwritten notes, images and documents and back up your files regularly.
► It is not so easy to look up something quickly if you've turned your computer off for the night and then think of something you want to check.

Choose software

The increasing range of genealogy software available can make it difficult to decide which one to choose. Here's a guide to some of the options.

Family Historian (www.family-historian. co.uk) A user-friendly software, which comes with a quick start printed manual as well as a more detailed electronic version. This is good for creating family trees, websites and CDs and for uploading pictures and other multimedia. There is a starter edition of the software on the CD-Rom in the back of the book.

Family Tree Maker (downloadable from www.ancestry.co.uk) This one has lots of features to help you create family trees and upload photographs and other multimedia.

Legacy Family Tree (www.legacyfamilytree. com) This is a good one to try out if you're uncertain about using software – the basic edition is free and can be downloaded from the website. You then have the option of paying to upgrade to the Deluxe version later if you want to – extra features include research help and advice, timelines and a publishing centre to create a book.

RootsMagic (www.rootsmagic. co.uk) An easy-to-use software programme that has lots of useful extra features, such as a web publishing wizard and help in creating a book to gather together all your research results. You can download a free 90-day trial from the website, so this is a good option if you're a bit nervous about using software.

Build Your Tree on a PC

FAMILY HISTORIAN STARTER EDITION 4.1 EXPLAINED

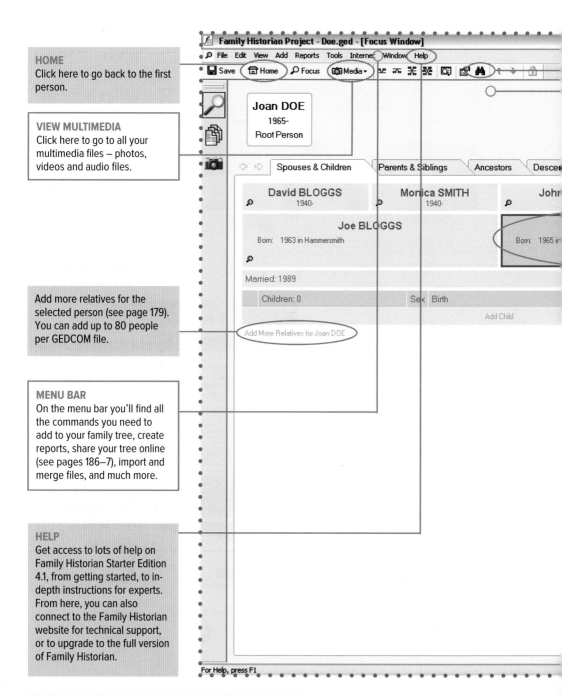

HOME
Click here to go back to the first person.

VIEW MULTIMEDIA
Click here to go to all your multimedia files – photos, videos and audio files.

Add more relatives for the selected person (see page 179). You can add up to 80 people per GEDCOM file.

MENU BAR
On the menu bar you'll find all the commands you need to add to your family tree, create reports, share your tree online (see pages 186–7), import and merge files, and much more.

HELP
Get access to lots of help on Family Historian Starter Edition 4.1, from getting started, to in-depth instructions for experts. From here, you can also connect to the Family Historian website for technical support, or to upgrade to the full version of Family Historian.

Family Historian Project - Doe.ged - [Focus Window]

File   Edit   View   Add   Reports   Tools   Internet   Window   Help

Save   Home   Focus   Media

Joan DOE
1965-
Root Person

Spouses & Children   Parents & Siblings   Ancestors   Descen

David BLOGGS   Monica SMITH   John
1940-   1940-

Joe BLOGGS
Born: 1963 in Hammersmith   Born: 1965 in

Married: 1989

Children: 0   Sex Birth
                                          Add Child

Add More Relatives for Joan DOE

For Help, press F1

Once you have installed Family Historian Starter Edition 4.1 from the CD-Rom in the back of the book (see page 224), and have created your first record (see pages 176–7), you will see this interface.

(see page 224)
(see pages 176–7)

SEARCH
You can search for names, families, sources and much more.

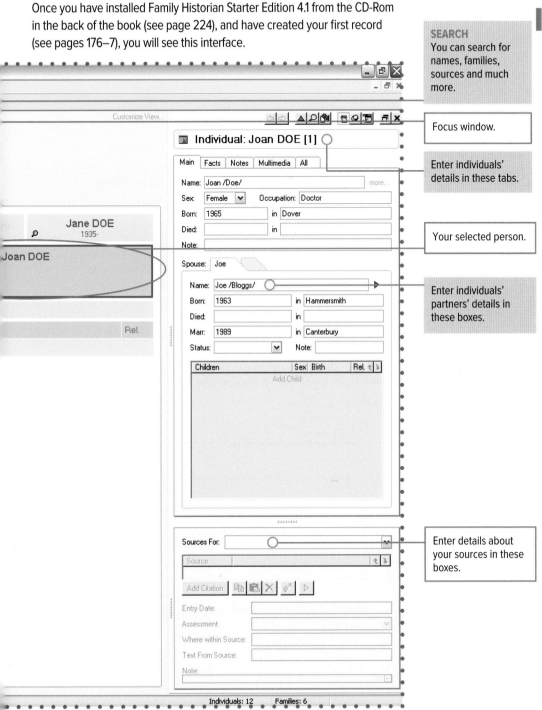

Customize View...

Individual: Joan DOE [1]

| Main | Facts | Notes | Multimedia | All |

Name: Joan /Doe/   more...
Sex: Female ▾   Occupation: Doctor
Born: 1965   in Dover
Died: in
Note:

Spouse: Joe

   Name: Joe /Bloggs/
   Born: 1963   in Hammersmith
   Died: in
   Marr: 1989   in Canterbury
   Status: ▾   Note:

   | Children | Sex | Birth | Rel. ↑↓ |
   Add Child

Sources For: ▾
Source   ↑↓

Add Citation 🗐 🗐 ✕ ℓ² ▷

Entry Date:
Assessment: ▾
Where within Source:
Text From Source:
Note:

Individuals: 12   Families: 6

Jane DOE
1935-

Joan DOE

Rel.

Focus window.

Enter individuals' details in these tabs.

Your selected person.

Enter individuals' partners' details in these boxes.

Enter details about your sources in these boxes.

USE SOFTWARE TO CREATE A FAMILY TREE

The CD-Rom in the back of the book contains family tree software, Family Historian Starter Edition 4.1. Once you have installed the software (see page 224), you can start building your family tree, adding up to 80 people per GEDCOM file, include photos and videos, and even make your own website (see pages 188–90). The following steps show you how to build a family tree using Family Historian Starter Edition 4.1.

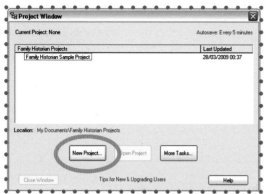

Start building your family tree

1 When you open Family Historian for the first time, click **New Project**

2 If you have previously built a family tree on your computer, you can import a GEDCOM file by clicking **Browse**, otherwise click **Next** to create the first record in your file

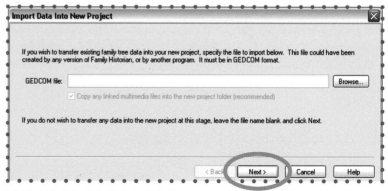

3 Type the person's name in the top box of the window that appears and then press the tab key on your keyboard, or click elsewhere to enter the information into the program's database. The last word of the name is assumed to be the surname and the software encloses it between forward slash (/) symbols. Other formats you have to edit manually, for example Walter/de la Mare/. Click **Next**

4 Enter a name for your project and check the 'Make default' box to ensure this project opens automatically each time you open the software

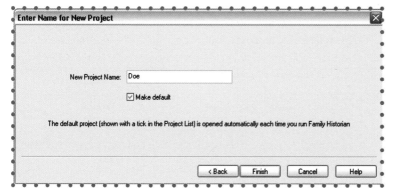

Next step ▶

GEDCOM is a universal file format that allows easy exchange of information between different software users. To find out more about GEDCOM, see pages 186–7.

5 Your project will now show in the 'Focus Window'

Add details

1 Click on the person you want to add details for to bring up a form in the right-hand panel. On the 'Main' tab, enter dates in the format 12 Jan 1956, although just the month and year, or just the year is OK

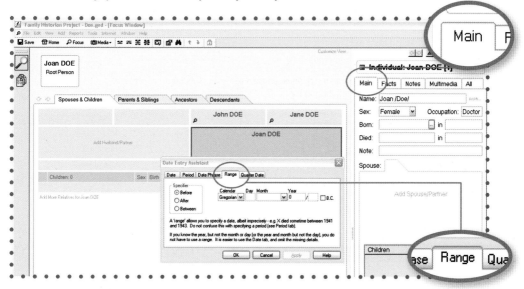

2 Click the button to the right of the box, and then the **Date** tab to add qualifiers such as 'approximate' and 'calculated', and the **Range** tab to add details to dates such as 'before', 'after' and 'between' two dates

3 Pressing the tab key takes you to the box associated with the date you have just entered. Type the location in full (for example 'Dover, Kent, England') as there are many programs that use your GEDCOM file to place your events and locations on to worldwide maps. It's good for cross-referencing purposes, too

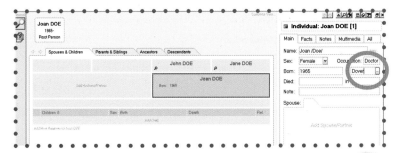

4 Click the **Show Sources** button to reveal a side panel showing any sources you have already linked to the selected event

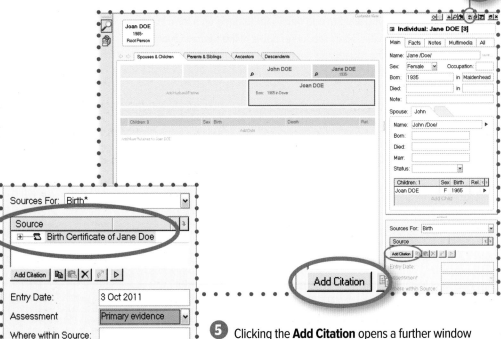

5 Clicking the **Add Citation** opens a further window showing all the sources you have already created. As this is your first one, click **New** to create it and enter at least its title, such as 'Birth Certificate of Jane Doe'

6 Your source will appear back in the main window. Add the 'Entry Date' and 'Assessment' (from 'Primary Evidence' to 'Unreliable'). For data from a large source, such as a book, you can quote the text and where in the source it is found

7 To add a spouse or partner, move to 'Spouse' and click **Add Spouse/ Partner**. This gives you the option to create a new person or a link to an existing person in your tree. In either case, the software automatically creates a marriage link for you

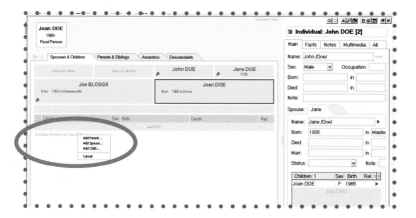

8 In the main part of the screen, double-click on the person you want to add more relatives for, in this case Joan Doe, then click **Add More Relatives for Joan Doe**

9 From the menu that pops up, you can then add parents, spouses or children. Complete the individual's details in the form on the right, as before

Apart from the 'Main' tab, there are several other places to add information about the person who is currently at the top of the window. Click the **Facts** tab, then **Add Fact** to add extra details, such as 'Baptism' or 'Emigration'. General notes about a person or family are entered on the 'Notes' tab.

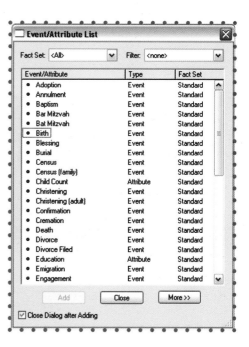

ADD MULTIMEDIA TO YOUR FAMILY TREE

Adding multimedia to a family tree, such as a photograph or an audio clip, helps to bring the past to life. Here's how to add a photographs in Family Historian Starter Edition 4.1.

1 To add a picture to the current person in your file, in the 'Focus Window' click the **Multimedia** tab and then click **Add Media**

2 In the pop-up window that appears click **Insert from File** and navigate to the image you want to add. Tick the 'Preview' option to see a thumbnail of the image. Click **Open** then **Copy** and the picture appears in the 'Edit Media Item' window for you to add a title, date and notes

3 To link the picture or sections within it to another person, double-click that person in the 'Focus Window'. In the **Multimedia** tab, click **Add Media**, then **Link to Existing Multimedia Record**. Find the image you want to link to in the left-hand pane, then click the **>** button to add it to the list on the right. Click **OK**. Click **Link to Face** then click and drag a box around one of the relevant faces in the picture. This face will now be linked to that person

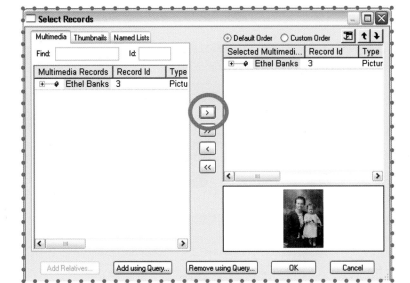

TRY THIS

Early photographs were often mounted on cards carrying the studio's name and address. To date a picture you can refer to local trade directories to see when the studio was in business.

4 Linking all the faces in a group picture to the people concerned is a handy way to identify each person. Click on the camera icon on the left side-bar to open a picture. As you move your mouse cursor over a picture the dotted boxes appear as they pass over each one. To identify a person click on a box and their name is highlighted on the left

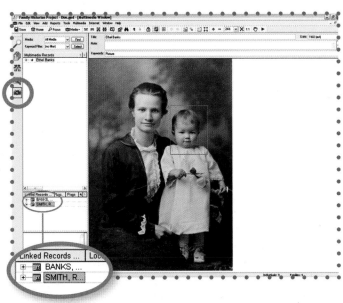

Build Your Tree on a PC

ONLINE FAMILY TREE BUILDERS

You can also build your family tree online. Genesreunited.co.uk is a good site to use, as it is free to register and screen prompts make creating your family tree very easy. One advantage of online family tree builders is that you can compare your tree to others (see page 184).

Build your family tree online

1 Go to **www.genesreunited.co.uk** and click **Register FREE**

2 On the next screen, enter the required details. Check whether you want the various options at the bottom of the screen; they automatically come with the boxes ticked, so make sure you are happy with these before continuing. Click **Register Free**

build your tree on a pc

3 For subsequent visits, you can just enter your email address and password, and the next screen will bring up any details you have already entered

4 Your name will automatically appear on the next screen. Click **Add Father** and a 'Quick Add' box will appear on your screen

5 Enter your father's details and click **Add Relation** to save these details. Repeat this process for your mother

6 Enter details for other members of the family, using the arrows that appear on the screen. Keep repeating this process until you have entered all the details you have

7 If you don't know exact details for any family member, enter approximate details, as you can amend the details later on using the 'Edit' button

8 An alternative to Steps 4–6 is to click **Family tree** on the menu at the top of the screen to open a screen giving options to 'Add Partner,' 'Add Child', 'Add Sibling', 'Add Father' and 'Add Mother'

Add photos

1 To add photos, select one of your relations, then click **Add a photo here**. Click **Find Files** in the dialog box that comes up

2 Find the photo you want to upload from among your computer's folders and files, then click **Send Files!**

Keep up to date

1 Somebody else may well be searching the same surname as you, and you might find you can make some links to your own family tree. Click **Search Trees** from the menu to see whether there are any matches among the family trees entered by other Genes Reunited members.

2 Every so often it's worth checking in 'Hot Matches'. Genes Reunited compares all family trees on the site and compares them to yours, with any matching names subsequently appearing in your Hot Matches section

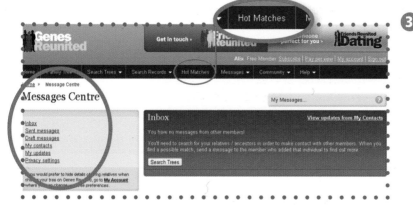

3 Check the 'Messages' section regularly, as members might try to contact you if they have spotted matches between your two family trees. The menu on the left of your screen has links to your 'Inbox', 'Sent Messages' and 'My contacts'

(4) In the 'Community' section, you will find the message board, where you can join in general genealogy discussions, help people who are looking for specific ancestors, or request information yourself about an elusive ancestor – someone may be able to help. You can also have a bit of fun with quizzes and games, make friends in the 'General Chat' section or read other people's success stories

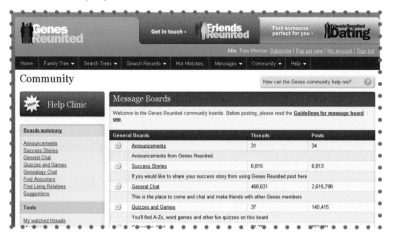

Share your family tree

(1) If you want to share your family tree online, you will need to pay a subscription. A standard subscription is currently £2.50 per month for six months, and allows you to exchange messages with other members and view their family trees when invited to do so

(2) Platinum membership is currently £8.33 per month for six months, and gives you access to extra records, including BMD indexes for England and Wales and overseas, as well as census records from 1841–1911

Top tips for sharing family trees online

▶ It is worth searching the site fairly regularly, as new members upload family trees all the time. A negative search one week might yield results two or three weeks later.

▶ If you are new to a website like this, before sending any messages look at other messages on the site to see how other people have done it. Decide which you think work the best and copy that format.

▶ When sending messages, put the family name you are searching for in upper case at the beginning of the message to stand the greatest chance of people spotting your message.

Build Your Tree on a PC

USE GEDCOM TO SHARE FAMILY TREES

GEDCOM (Genealogical Data Communication) is a universal file format that allows easy exchange of information between different software users. If you use Family Historian Starter Edition 4.1, then GEDCOM is built into the program. But if your software uses a different format, you will be able to convert files to GEDCOM online.

Create a GEDCOM file

1 Go to **www.genesreunited.com** and click **Family Tree** and then **Import GEDCOM**

BE CAREFUL

While you can select a folder from an external hard drive, folders on most removable media devices – such as CDs, DVDs and some USB sticks – can't be included in a library.

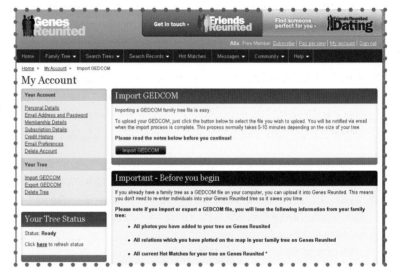

2 From the menu on the left, under 'Your tree' click **Export GEDCOM**. Then on the next screen click again on **Export GEDCOM**. Your family tree will be emailed to you as an attachment and you can then edit it offline and email to family and friends

Receiving a GEDCOM file

When you receive an email notifying you about a family tree containing a GEDCOM file you can do one of two things:

1 If you are using Family Historian Starter Edition 4.1, double click on the file and it will open in the software

2 If using other software, click **Import** to convert the GEDCOM file into a format compatible with your own software

Merge a GEDCOM file

If the GEDCOM file contains information relevant to your family research, you will want to merge it with the information in your own database. In Family Historian Starter Edition 4.1:

1 Make back-up files of your own database, in case something goes wrong. On the menu bar, click **File**, then **Backup/Restore**, then **Backup**. Give your back-up file a name and browse to where you want to save it. Choose to save either as a zip file or a GEDCOM file

2 Make sure you are happy to merge the files, as a merge cannot be undone. To import the file, click **File**, then **Merge/Compare File....** Browse your computer to find the file you want to merge, click **Open**. Choose whether you want the software to suggest candidate matches for merging, or not to match any records

3 Follow the instructions on screen to choose which individuals, families, multimedia and sources to merge. Click **Help** at any point to bring up detailed instructions on each step of the merge

BE CAREFUL

Once you have sent someone a GEDCOM file, you have no control over what they do with the information. So think very carefully what information you are happy to share with people and what you would prefer to keep private. Most software programs have the facility to filter out living people, so you only share information about ancestors who are no longer alive.

build your tree on a pc

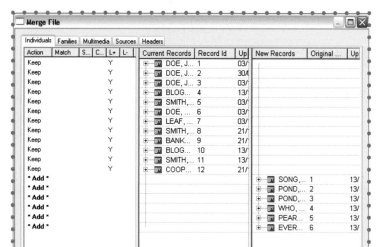

CREATE YOUR OWN WEBSITE

Another way of sharing your family tree online is to create your own website. This can be a wonderful way of presenting your findings and you can give your imagination free reign and be as creative and artistic as you like. Family members will love reading about shared relatives and looking at their photos and other memorabilia that you can photograph and upload to your website. If you shudder at the thought of setting up your own website, don't – it really isn't as complicated as you think it is.

Advantages
▶ It's an easy way for family members to access your family history research.
▶ Reading your website might jog people's memories and they can contribute to the site.
▶ You can have a lot of fun with it.

Disadvantages
▶ You have to bear the brunt of any costs and technical problems, so this may not be the best option for you.
▶ It can be very time-consuming, so it might not be a good option if you don't have a lot of spare time.

Create your own website using Family Historian Starter Edition 4.1

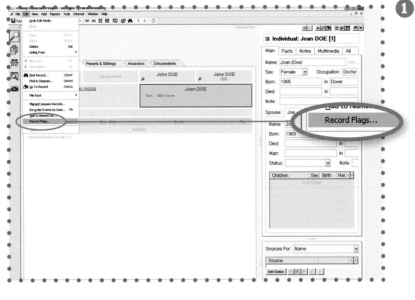

1 On the top menu bar, click **Internet** then **Create a Website** to open the wizard that leads you through the stages to create a finished site. The first step gives you the option to withhold information about individuals marked with a 'Private' flag – flags are set for each person on the 'Edit' menu, then click **Record Flags**

2 You can also choose to include minimal information for those with a 'Living' or 'Private' flag

3 Click **Next** to select who is in your website. Click **Add All** to include everybody, or **Select** to open a new window that lists the people in your file on the left and the ones you select from the list on the right. Click **Next**

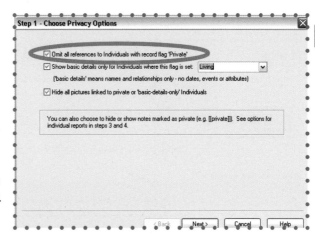

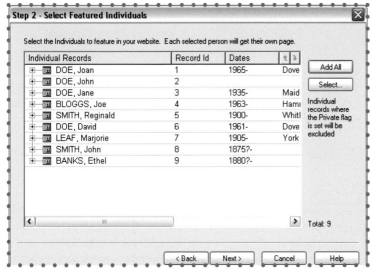

4 Pick the main type of report to be used in the website from the 'Primary Page Type' drop-down list. If you choose the default 'Family Group Sheet' (for Web or CD), you will have to select 'Individual Summary Report' (for Web or CD) in the secondary field to cater for people who never married

5 Next to each selection are the 'Options' buttons that open a new window offering selections on five tabs for 'Contents', 'Pictures', 'Sources', 'Format' and 'Page Layout'. Once you have made all your selections, click **OK** then **Next**

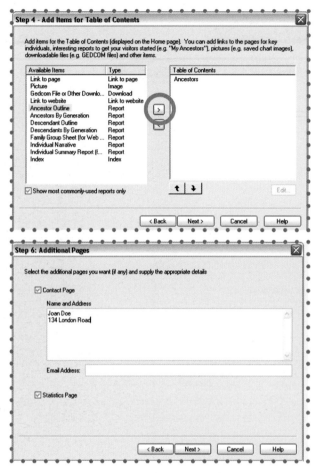

6 Your home page welcomes visitors to your site, so it's important to add a picture, a link to a general report about the family or a link to another website to make it eye-catching for visitors. Select these items in the left-hand window and move them across with the > button. Next add a title for your home page. Click **Select** to navigate to a picture you may want to include – you can add a caption in the box provided. Below this there is space to type your own message to welcome visitors. Click **Next**

7 In the next two windows add your contact details and add your own logo, or keep the default one at the top of each page

8 Pages display any text you enter in 'Header Text.' Use the 'Colours' button to set the colour of each element on the page

9 Select a folder in which to store the files and click **Finish** to create and store them. Click the **View Website** button to see it in your default web browser or use the adjacent button for advice on how to upload it to the internet

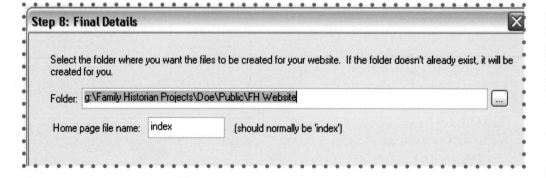

GENEALOGY FRIENDS ONLINE

By reading and following all the steps in this chapter, you will learn how to:

▶ **Use the internet to share information, ideas and tips with other family history researchers**

▶ **Use mailing lists, web forums and blogs to help your research**

▶ **Use social networking sites to share information and find friends and relatives**

JOIN A MAILING LIST

A mailing list is an email exchange forum for people interested in the same topic. You can subscribe to the list free of charge to send and receive emails.

Advantages

▶ They can help you to find answers to specific problems and engage in online discussions with like-minded people.

▶ You can offer help to others.

▶ You can find yourself making friends with fellow 'listers'. It has been known for members of mailing lists to meet up and even finish up getting married – but don't join just for that reason!

Disadvantages

▶ You can find yourself inundated with unwanted emails, but if people use the subject line sensibly it should be fairly easy to scan through to see which interest you, and delete the rest.

▶ Online discussions can occasionally get heated. For a peaceful life, don't get involved – just ignore them.

Find a mailing list

1 On **www.rootsweb.com**, select **Mailing Lists**

TRY THIS

If your email program has the facility, create a separate folder for your mailing list (or several folders if you are joining several lists) and then set up a filter so that all mailing list emails go into the appropriate folders. This avoids cluttering up your main inbox.

2 On the next screen, you can search current mailing lists or the mailing list archives using keywords – for example, a surname or an occupation

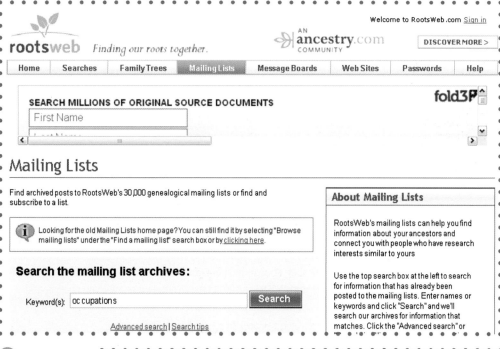

Welcome to RootsWeb.com Sign in

rootsweb *Finding our roots together.*   ⊲| AN **ancestry**.com COMMUNITY   DISCOVER MORE >

| Home | Searches | Family Trees | Mailing Lists | Message Boards | Web Sites | Passwords | Help |

SEARCH MILLIONS OF ORIGINAL SOURCE DOCUMENTS   fold3P

First Name

Mailing Lists

Find archived posts to RootsWeb's 30,000 genealogical mailing lists or find and subscribe to a list.

ⓘ Looking for the old Mailing Lists home page? You can still find it by selecting "Browse mailing lists" under the "Find a mailing list" search box or by clicking here.

Search the mailing list archives:

Keyword(s): occupations   Search

Advanced search | Search tips

About Mailing Lists

RootsWeb's mailing lists can help you find information about your ancestors and connect you with people who have research interests similar to yours

Use the top search box at the left to search for information that has already been posted to the mailing lists. Enter names or keywords and click "Search" and we'll search our archives for information that matches. Click the "Advanced search" or

3 For example, entering 'Occupations' brings up the list shown

Welcome to RootsWeb.com Sign in

rootsweb *Finding out roots together.*   ⊲| AN **ancestry**.com COMMUNITY   DISCOVER MORE >

| Home | Searches | Family Trees | Mailing Lists | Message Boards | Web Sites | Passwords | Help |

SEARCH MILLIONS OF ORIGINAL SOURCE DOCUMENTS   fold3P

First Name

Find a List Search

Viewing **1-25** of **84** matches from **32,133** mailing lists

List Name	Description	Location	Sur
OCCUPATIONS			
REMOTE-WORK			
DOCTORS-NURSES-MIDWIVES			
CANAL-PEOPLE	canal workers and barge owners.		
PIRATES	For anyone with a genealogical or historical interest... more		
INDIAN-TRADERS		USA	
HM-CUSTOMS-WATERGUARD			HM-CUSTOMS-WAT
PAPER-MILLS-MAKERS	paper mills and paper makers.		
CIRCUS-FOLK	A mailing list for anyone with a genealogical interest... more		
BRITISH-MARINERS	Genealogical discussions of information pertaining... more		
RIC	A mailing list for anyone with a genealogical... more		
MUSIC-OCCUPATIONS	A mailing list for anyone with a genealogical interest... more		
HUCKSTERS-AND-TEAMSTERS	A mailing list for anyone with a genealogical... more		
GLSHIPS	anyone who is researching ancestors who participated... more		
COALMINERS	anyone whose ancestors were coalminers in the... more		
LONGHUNTERS	the longhunters, indian traders, and the "overhill"... more		
WYMING	miners and the mining industry in Wyoming.	USA, Wyoming	
FURTRAPPERS-MOUNTAINMEN	A mailing list for anyone with a genealogical... more		
THEATRICAL-ANCESTORS	A mailing list for anyone who is researching ancestors... more		
CA-HISTORY-HYDRAULIC-MINING		USA, California	
SCOTTISH-MINING	A mailing list for anyone who with a genealogical... more	Scotland	

Genealogy Friends Online

4 Select from this list – for example, you might have ancestors who worked on the canals, so select the **Canal-People** mailing list

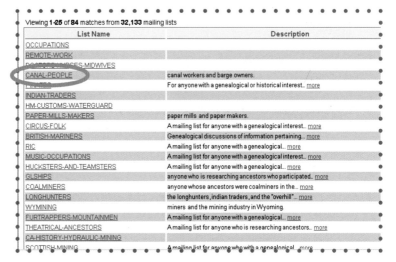

5 You can then choose to subscribe to the mailing list should you so desire (see opposite). You can also unsubscribe whenever you choose and search and browse the archives

Occupations: CANAL-PEOPLE Mailing List

CANAL-PEOPLE-L
lists9

Topic: canal workers and barge owners.

For questions about this list, contact the list administrator at CANAL-PEOPLE-admin@rootsweb.com

- **Subscribing.** Clicking on one of the shortcut links below should work, but if your browser doesn't understand them, try these manual instructions: to join **CANAL-PEOPLE-L**, send mail to CANAL-PEOPLE-L-request@rootsweb.com with the single word *subscribe* in the message subject and body. To join **CANAL-PEOPLE-D**, do the same thing with CANAL-PEOPLE-D-request@rootsweb.com
    - Subscribe to CANAL-PEOPLE-L
    - Subscribe to CANAL-PEOPLE-D (digest)
- **Unsubscribing.** To leave **CANAL-PEOPLE-L**, send mail to CANAL-PEOPLE-L-request@rootsweb.com with the single word *unsubscribe* in the message subject and body. To leave **CANAL-PEOPLE-D**, do the same thing with CANAL-PEOPLE-D-request@rootsweb.com
    - Unsubscribe from CANAL-PEOPLE-L
    - Unsubscribe from CANAL-PEOPLE-D (digest)
- **Archives.** You can search the archives for a specific message or browse them, going from one message to another. Some list archives are not available; if there is a link here to an archive but the link doesn't work, it probably just means that no messages have been posted to that list yet.
    - Search the CANAL-PEOPLE archives
    - Browse the CANAL-PEOPLE archives

Join a mailing list

1 Most are free to join – simply select the one that interests you and then click **Subscribe**

2 An email opens automatically – type 'Subscribe' in the 'Subject' line and click **Send**

3 You should receive an email more or less straightaway, confirming your membership and giving information about how to use the list. It is worth reading through this, even if you are familiar with using mailing lists, as it might have some useful hints and tips

4 To unsubscribe, send an email with 'Unsubscribe' in the 'Subject' line and you should receive another confirmation email

Which mode to subscribe to?
Mailing lists come in two modes:

Mail mode, where you receive emails as they are posted.
Digest mode, where you receive a batch of recent emails in one post, usually weekly.

Tips for sending messages to mailing lists
▶ Make sure your subject line is as clear and precise about the contents of the email as possible, as it is more likely to be noticed by people who can help. Avoid long subject lines if you can.
▶ Consider whether your reply will be of interest to the list as a whole, or whether it would be more appropriate just to respond to the person who sent the original message.
▶ Avoid quoting entire emails, posting emails on subjects that are irrelevant to that list, and being impolite or abusive – otherwise you will incur the wrath of the list owner.

genealogy friends online

BE CAREFUL
Should you receive abusive posts, forward them on to the list owner, who will deal with them. Don't be tempted to deal with them yourself, or get involved in an argument.

Genealogy Friends Online

WEB FORUMS

These are single subject areas online where members can post messages and files. These can be invaluable for sharing and requesting information about your ancestors. You don't need to subscribe. Newsgroups are similar in that they provide the facility to post message onto an online message board.

Advantages

▶ Unlike mailing lists, you don't receive loads of emails.
▶ The only emails you will receive are those alerting you to the fact that one of your postings to the forum has elicited a response.

Disadvantages

▶ You need to remember to check the message board regularly if you have posted a message requesting information, so that you don't miss anything.
▶ Forums don't always have the same feel as a mailing list.

Join an online forum

1 On the home page of a website such as www.rootschat.com, register free. On subsequent visits, you will need to log in

---

RootsChat.com

Welcome, **Guest**. Please login or register
Did you miss your activation email?
Monday 12 September 11 15:53 BST (UK)

Login

Welcome Forum Help Surnames Library Shop Search Login Register

Ads by Google   Family History   England Genealogy   Genealogy History   Lancashire Genealogy   Yorkshire Genealogy
Parish Records Online Search Millions of Parish Records Official Documents from the UK Find-mypast.co.uk/Parish Records
Ireland Family History Records 4,000,000,000+ Names. Hurry-Find Your Ancestors Now! www.FamilyLink.com/Ireland
Family Law Goodwins Family Law In Harrow Experience & Expertise. goodwinsfamilylaw.co.uk

AdChoices ▷

News:

Register – it's **totally free** to register and use RootsChat.

Choose username:
This will be your displayed name while on RootsChat. It is best not to use your full name incase of identity fraud.

which

Email:
This must be a valid email address, as RootsChat will send you a confirmation email.

Choose password:

Verify password:

Please enter the code as shown:

0 ' C B 5

You must read and type the **6 chars** within **0..9** and **A..F**

YOUR EMAIL ADDRESS WILL BE KEPT HIDDEN FROM OTHERS.

WE VERY STONGLY ENCOURAGE YOU NOT TO DISCLOSE YOUR EMAIL ADDRESS FOR PUBLICATION ON ANY WEBSITE

ROOTSCHAT MEMBERS CAN STILL CONTACT YOU SAFELY WITHOUT THE RISK OF VIRUSES OR UNSOLICITED (SPAM) EMAILS

You agree, through your use of this **RootsChat** forum and Chatroom, that you will not post any material which is false, defamatory, inaccurate, abusive, vulgar, hateful, harassing, obscene, profane, sexually oriented, threatening, invasive of a living person's privacy, or otherwise contrary to law. Legal actions can be taken against you. You also agree not to post any copyrighted material unless the copyright is owned by you or you have consent from the owner of the copyrighted material. You acknowledge that you alone will be responsible for breaches of copyright. By posting look-ups you acknowledge you are the copyright owner, entitled to disclose the information, or the material is not covered by copyright. Spam, flooding, advertisements except in the "For Sale/Wanted/Events" Forum, chain letters, pyramid schemes, and solicitations are

2 On the home page you can instantly see some of the most current topics under discussion. Scroll through and see if any interest you; if so, just click on the topic and you can start sending and receiving posts straightaway

[Travelling People]	Interesting traveller names! by Redroger **Today** at 15:50:52
[The Common Room]	Finding Carlie - help please. by Daisy Loo **Today** at 15:50:38
[Hertfordshire]	CAINS family of Ippollitts and Barnet by kerry1212 **Today** at 15:48:57
[Hertfordshire]	Occupation: Oil Cake Trimmer by Redroger **Today** at 15:48:50
[Beginners]	Harold Derbyshire 1896? by lin46 **Today** at 15:47:26
[The Common Room]	Unfortunate names found in family trees? by rachelralph **Today** at 15:47:16
[Yorkshire (West Riding)]	Slackthwaite, Slaigthwaite, Slaithwaite, Parack, Booth by Sunlaws **Today** at 15:46:50
[Kent]	Can't find him in 1901 census but have his marriage in 1902! by westwood1 **Today** at 15:46:34
[Canada]	Clezie - Clazey - Clazie in Montréal, 1830s by cosmac **Today** at 15:44:28
[Scotland - General]	Scottish ancestors at Battle of Worcester 1651? by bruce1746 **Today** at 15:44:19
[Leicestershire]	School / University records for Leicester? by diddymiller **Today** at 15:43:37
[Scotland - General]	Succesion Lairs Scotland - Advice by Falkyrn **Today** at 15:41:06
[Suffolk]	John MAYHEW, Francis HUBBARD, James BARRITT/BARRETT - Suffolk Families by deon **Today** at 15:40:11
[Durham]	Ann Pickering by kerry1212 **Today** at 15:39:01
[Armed Forces]	british army involvement in russian civil war 1919 by Maryan **Today** at 15:39:01
[London & Middlesex Lookup Requests]	Probate/Wills Middlesex by carol8353 **Today** at 15:38:04
[Deciphering & Recognition Help]	A Hospital in Manchester, England by Phodgetts **Today** at 15:37:35
[Australia]	Sweden Place Name by BatUser **Today** at 15:37:04
[Cumberland Lookup Requests]	Thomas Davidson by emmsthheight **Today** at 15:35:57
[Europe]	Sweden Place Name by Britt **Today** at 15:35:41
[Warwickshire Lookup Requests]	Elizabeth Burbidge by karl sollis **Today** at 15:34:55
[Other Countries]	George Harrision Townshend by startt **Today** at 15:31:36
[Gloucestershire Lookup Requests]	william williams by kenandjulie **Today** at 15:31:24
[Buckinghamshire]	West Wycombe Parish Registers by edencars **Today** at 15:31:04
[Canada Lookup Request]	Meugens family by Jacquie in Canada **Today** at 15:30:13
[Leicestershire]	Is Woodhouse in Leicestershire? by Mike from Leicester **Today** at 15:30:01
[World War One]	Army Reserve by jds1949 **Today** at 15:29:26
[Wiltshire Lookup Requests]	Relationship by Cumbrian Nige **Today** at 15:29:26

3 Alternatively, if you scroll down to the bottom of the screen, you can select an area of interest. This will take you through to the message board relating to that topic

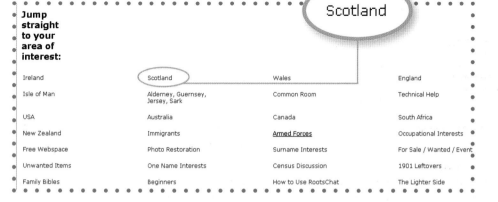

Jump straight to your area of interest:

Scotland

Ireland	Scotland	Wales	England
Isle of Man	Alderney, Guernsey, Jersey, Sark	Common Room	Technical Help
USA	Australia	Canada	South Africa
New Zealand	Immigrants	Armed Forces	Occupational Interests
Free Webspace	Photo Restoration	Surname Interests	For Sale / Wanted / Event
Unwanted Items	One Name Interests	Census Discussion	1901 Leftovers
Family Bibles	Beginners	How to Use RootsChat	The Lighter Side

4 Another way in is to click **Enter RootsChat** at the top of the screen, and choose from the selection of topics, such as Scotland

5 You will be presented with another list of topics relating to that subject. Click on one that interests you so that you can start reading and responding to messages

Links to other local history or genealogy websites of interest		397	915	in Ancestral Atlas by sdbadger
For Sale / Wanted / Events Genealogical and Family History items 'For Sale' and 'Wanted' (this includes private and commercial posts), and details of any Family History or Local History Fairs or other Events of genealogical interest.		1265	1880	Yesterday at 17:50:35 in Schneider Trophy Exhibit... by Bilge
Ireland (Historical Counties)				
Ireland - General Irish family history not specific to a county. *Moderators: KarenM, heywood, aghudovey, shanew147* *Child Boards: Antrim, Armagh, Carlow, Cavan, Clare, Cork, Derry (Londonderry), Donegal, Down, Dublin, Fermanagh, Galway, Kerry, Kildare, Kilkenny, Leois (Queens), Leitrim, Limerick, Longford, Louth, Mayo, Meath, Monaghan, Offaly (Kings), Roscommon, Sligo, Tipperary, Tyrone, Waterford, Westmeath, Wexford, Wicklow*		3754	23970	Today at 15:30:46 in Re: Burka wild geese fro... by leprechaun
Ireland Resources All those great Irish resources for family history and local history. *Moderators: KarenM, heywood, aghudovey, shanew147*		86	600	Yesterday at 07:03:31 in Re: Irish Prison Records... by Ann in the UK
Irish Language Posts in this section to be in Gaeilge (Gaelge) . Posts in English will be deleted. *Moderator: RootsChat*		10	76	Wednesday 06 July 11 22:12 BST (UK) in Re: Taiféid an RIC le fo... by eadaoin
Scotland (Counties as in 1851-1901)				
Scotland - General Scottish family history not specific to a county. *Moderators: Monical, ev* *Child Boards: Aberdeenshire, Angus (Forfarshire), Argyllshire, Ayrshire, Banffshire, Berwickshire, Buteshire, Caithness, Clackmannanshire, Dumfriesshire, Dunbartonshire, East Lothian (Haddingtonshire), Fife, Inverness, Kincardineshire, Kinross-shire, Kirkcudbrightshire, Lanarkshire, Midlothian, Moray (Elginshire), Nairnshire, Orkney, Peeblesshire, Perthshire, Renfrewshire, Ross & Cromarty, Roxburghshire, Selkirkshire, Shetland, Stirlingshire, Sutherland, West Lothian (Linlithgowshire), Wigtownshire*		3397	283	Today at 15:29:31 in Re: Grays from Cambusnet... by snooki
Scotland Resources Resources for research in Scotland: Links, Books, Archives, etc. *Moderators: Monical, ev*		149	365	Sunday 23 October 11 BST (UK) in Re: Scotsfind.org offin... by hissafer
Gaelic Language Posts in this section to be in Gaelic only. Posts in English will be deleted. *Moderator: RootsChat*		6	28	Sunday 30 November 08 18:57 GMT (UK) in San Aindrias by eadaoin
Wales (Counties as in 1851-1901)				
Wales - General Welsh family history not specific to a county. *Moderator: RootsChat* *Child Boards: Anglesey, Breconshire, Caernarvonshire, Cardiganshire, Carmarthenshire, Denbighshire, Flintshire, Glamorganshire, Merionethshire, Monmouthshire, Montgomeryshire, Pembrokeshire, Radnorshire*		1066	7167	Today at 14:36:26 in Re: william stephen mati... by gwen j
Wales Resources		38	142	in WERN CHAPEL REGISTERS, W...

6 On every list of topics, there are columns on the right telling you how many posts there are relating to this topic, and when the last message was posted – this will give you an idea of how recent the discussion is

7 On most sites you can also upload images and files to share with members, and perhaps give help with providing missing information or identifying pictures

8 Most sites also give links to other family history websites

TIP

If there is a help section, it's worth having a look at this before you get started, even if you are familiar with forums, as there will be some useful information about using the particular website.

Websites with forums

Below is a selection of the most popular websites with genealogy forums:

www.rootschat.com
www.british-genealogy.com/forums
www.genforum.genealogy.com
www.ancestry.com/share
www.talkingscot.com (for Scottish ancestry discussions)

BLOGGING

Another way to share findings with others is to create your own blog. Blogs are extremely popular these days, so you might well attract a good number of like-minded people to yours.

Advantages

▶ Anyone can read your blog and leave comments and useful information relating to your research.

Disadvantages

▶ You need to update regularly or readers will lose interest. So this is not a good option if you don't have a lot of time to spare.

▶ People might leave comments you don't like. Unless they are constructive criticism, it's best just to ignore them.

Setting up a blog is easy. There's lots of blogging software available, and one of the most popular and free to use is Google Blogger.

Jargon buster

Blog
An abbreviation of 'web log', a blog is an online journal used for all sorts of subjects.

genealogy friends online

Get started

1 To use Blogger, you must first create a free Google account. Click **Create a Google Account** on the top-right corner of any Google webpage and enter a username and a password

2 Type 'www.blogger.com' into the address bar of your web browser. Once the Blogger home page is loaded, enter your username and password (see Step 1), and click **Sign in**

3 Enter a display name (this will be what people will see) and click **Create a Blog**. On the next screen, click **Start Blogging**

④ You need to pick a title and web address (URL) for your blog. Type a name, such as 'My Family History' into the box next to the blog title

⑤ In the blog address (URL) box, type in a word. Click the **Check Availability** link to see if you can use that word in your blog URL address

⑥ You'll also be able to choose a template, which will determine how your blog will look when it's published. From the range of templates, you can click the **Preview template** link to see how your blog pages will look. Click a template name to use it for your blog design, then click **Continue**

Create the look of your blog

You can edit this default template at any stage to customise the look of your blog or simply change it to another template entirely by using Blogger's Dashboard.

① Click **Dashboard** from the top right of the page. Click to bring up the following editing options: **Page Elements**, **Edit HTML** and **Template Designer**

② **Page Elements** may be of most interest at this stage, as it allows you to rearrange the elements of your Blogger site by dragging and dropping them around your site. You can also add other sections to your page. Sections include **About Me**, **Blog Archive** and **Followers**. These can be helpful to readers – the Blog Archive will, for example, allow visitors to see older blog posts that you have previously made

3 In **Page Elements** will be a range of gadgets you can add to your site, by clicking the **Add a Gadget** link. Gadgets can include the ability to search YouTube or view your Gmail inbox. There are thousands of gadgets to choose from, but clicking **Most Popular** will give you a good idea of what other bloggers find most useful

Customise your Blogger profile

1 Before you start blogging, you may want to add to your profile. Click the **Dashboard** link in the top right-hand corner of your Blogger home page

2 Click **Edit Profile** and fill in the fields on the **User Profile** page. Click **Save Profile**. Return to the Dashboard by clicking on **Dashboard**

3 Click the **Create your Blog Now** button. You're now ready to add your first blog entry

Start writing

1 Click the **New Post** button and you'll be presented with a page that works in a similar way to a word-processing program, complete with all the usual text formatting options.

2 Each blog entry should have a title – enter a title for your entry in the **Title** field, and type your entry in the empty text field. Enhance text with the formatting options. You can also click the **Preview** button to see how any formatting will appear on the published page

3 When you're happy with your entry, click **Publish Post** at the foot of the page. You are now an official blogger

Promoting your blog

After taking the trouble to write a blog, most people want it to be viewed by as many people as possible, and there are Blogger settings designed to promote your efforts.

TRY THIS

Email your family and any other contacts made on mailing lists and discussion forums to tell them about your blog. The more the word spreads, the more visits you will get and the more likely you are to attract people who can help with information.

genealogy friends online

Make sure you 'ping'

You need your blog to 'ping' (ie make contact with) other sites, because this means it will be included in various 'recently updated' lists on the web as well as other blog-related services.

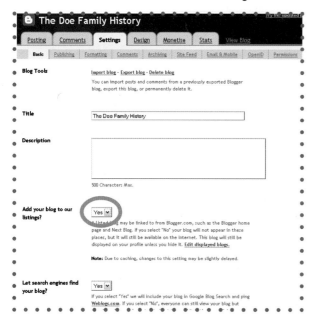

1 To do this, you need to enable two key settings. Click **Dashboard**, then **Settings** then **Basic**

2 Click **Add your blog to our listings**. This determines whether or not the Blogger home page, Blogger Play, will link to your blog

3 Click **Let search engines find your blog?** This determines whether your blog will be included in Google Blog Search, and if it will ping Weblogs.com. If you select **No**, everyone can still view your blog, but search engines will be instructed not to list it in their search results

Feed reader software

Enabling your Blogger site to take advantage of 'feed reader' software is another good way to get your blog out there. A site feed means that it can be picked up and displayed on other websites and information aggregation tools, called aggregators. These scan your site feed and automatically let your readers know when your blog has been updated. An example of such software is Google Reader, which you can use with your Google Account.

1 In your Google Account, go to **Settings** then **Site Feed**

2 You'll have one simple option of how much of your content you want to syndicate. Choosing **Full** will put the entire content of each post in your site feed; choosing **Short** includes only an excerpt from the beginning of each post. Choosing the **None** option turns your site feed off entirely

3 In **Advanced Mode** there are options for three different types of feeds. The first is for your blog posts, and is the same as the single option in **Basic Mode**. After that comes the comment feed that contains all comments made on all posts on your blog. Finally, there is the pre-post comment feed. With this option, each post will have its

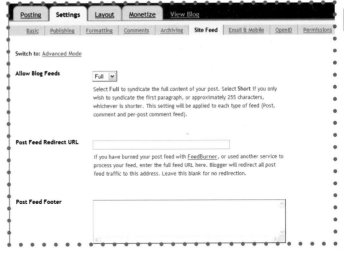

own site feed, containing only its own comments. Each option has the same **Full**, **Short** and **None** setting choices

Other blogging websites

www.typepad.com For this you get a 30-day trial, then you have to pay to continue using it

www.blog.com A basic free service, with a choice of upgrades that you have to pay for

www.cyndislist.com/blogs.htm A useful list of other people's blogs to give you inspiration.

SOCIAL NETWORKING SITES

This is another great way to link up with people who share your interests as well as with relatives.

Advantages

▶ You get to 'meet' new people who share your interests.

▶ You can share information and pictures.

▶ They are a great way to stay in touch with family members who are also researching your ancestry, and with distant relatives, perhaps those living in a different country.

Disadvantages

▶ Users of social network sites often try to attract as many 'friends' as possible, so you might find yourself getting inundated with requests from people you don't know and who don't share your interests. So be very selective about which personal details you put online.

Which site?

On most sites you can do more or less the same things – invite friends to join by entering their email addresses, and upload photos, videos, sound clips and news to share with family and friends. For most you need to register to use the site to its full extent. Popular social networking sites include:

Facebook – www.facebook.com Facebook's popularity continues to grow worldwide. It's a site designed to help you find and keep in touch with friends. It is easy to navigate through the busy site and, once connected, to see what friends are doing. It offers various privacy settings on the site to protect users' information. (See pages 206–8 for information on setting up your own Facebook page.)

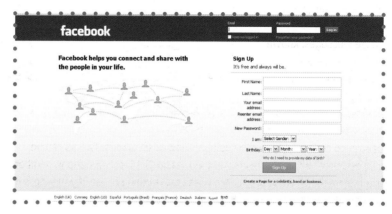

Flickr – www.flickr.com Flickr is a photo-sharing website that has established a strong following among those keen to show off their photography skills. Free account holders can upload 100MB of photos and videos to share, and can join in discussion groups and send messages to other users. It lacks sophisticated features, but is easy to use and allows you to restrict who can see your information.

Sagazone – www.sagazone.co.uk This is a social network site run by Saga Group and specifically aimed at the over-50s market. The site lacks many of the advanced features found on sites like Facebook, but its carefully chosen demographic means it attracts a large number of like-minded people. Signing up to the website is a little convoluted but, overall, it is simple and well-signposted.

Twitter – www.twitter. com A great way to stay up to date with friends and other people you are interested in is via Twitter – a site that allows its users to send and read text-based messages of up to 140 characters. These messages, known as Tweets, are displayed on your profile page and delivered to your friends, who are known as 'followers'. You can restrict delivery to certain people or, by default, allow open access. Tweets can be sent and received via the Twitter website, a text (SMS) on your phone or other external methods. While the service itself costs nothing to use, if you access it on your phone you may incur phone service provider fees.

Genealogy Friends Online

SET UP A FACEBOOK ACCOUNT

Facebook is one of the biggest and most popular social networking sites and is a great way to keep in touch with friends and relatives.

1 To join Facebook, type **www.facebook.com** into the address bar of your web browser. Once the page is loaded, you should register. Registering means choosing a username and entering a valid email address. You'll need these each time you log in

2 Complete your Facebook registration by clicking on the link sent by Facebook to your email

3 You will be asked to fill out your 'Profile information' as well as uploading a photo or taking one with your webcam. You can skip both these stages if you wish

4 Facebook will now invite you to locate friends on the site by entering your email address and password. It will search your email for names that appear in its own database and, if found, will then show their account details. Most of the popular webmail services can be searched, including Gmail, Hotmail and AOL

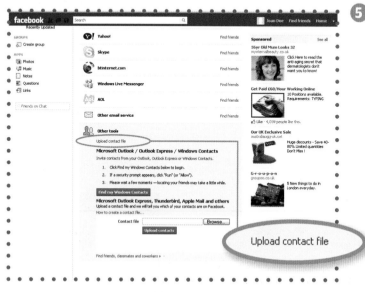

5 The 'Find Friends' feature also lets you locate people with the email program you use on your PC. To do this, click **Upload contact file** and then, depending on what email program you use, click **Find my Windows Contacts**, or browse to find a contact file and click **Upload contacts**. If you're unsure how to locate a contact file for the email program you use, click **How to create a contact file**. This lists 10 of the leading email programs. Click the name of the one you use to bring up a step-by-step guide

6 In 'Find Friends' you can search for old school friends or co-workers. In the 'Friends' panel, click **Other tools**. Click **Find friends, classmates and coworkers** to search for people you might know. You can search by hometown, current location, secondary school, college or university, employer and university (postgraduate)

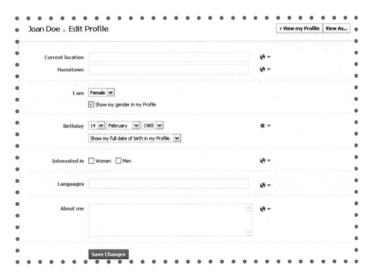

Search for other friends

You can also search for people by typing a name into the search box at the top of the page. When you come across someone you'd like to be a friend, click the **Add friend** button.

Edit your profile

1 Your Facebook profile shows who you are, with sections including 'Basic Information', 'Work and Education' and 'Contact Information'. Though there's no obligation to do so, filling these in will make it easier for other people to find you on Facebook. Click on your name in the top right menu bar and then click **Edit My Profile**

2 Adding a profile picture also makes it easier for friends to identify you, especially if you have a common name. To add a profile picture, click on your name in the top right menu bar and then click **Edit My Profile**. Click **Profile picture** in the left-hand menu. You can then browse for a picture on your computer, or take one if you have a webcam.

207

Genealogy Friends Online

Write something

1 On your 'Wall' page, you can publish your status – how you're feeling, what you're up to – photos, notes and more. This comes in the form of a text box at the top of your page, below your name, just above the 'stream' of information

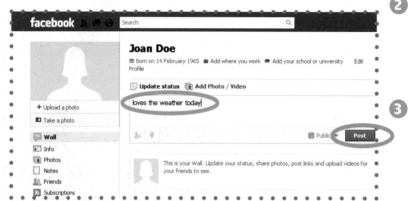

2 Clicking inside the text box also displays other types of content you can share

3 Once you've added content, click **Post**. Your posts will now show up on your 'Wall' and on your friends' Home pages

4 You have two streams. One is your 'Wall', which is in your profile area (click on your name on the menu bar and then **Wall**) and the other is the 'News Feed' on your 'Home' page (click **Home** on the menu bar, then **News Feed**). These represent the ongoing conversations between you and your friends. The 'Wall' is a space on each user's profile page that lets friends post messages (these can be seen by other friends), while the 'News Feed' highlights information such as profile changes and birthdays and shows conversations taking place on friends' walls

5 On the left-hand side of your 'Home' page is a panel of 'filters' that

allow you to determine what kind of content you see in your two streams at any given time. The options include 'Photos', 'Notes' and 'Music'. Clicking a filter brings up options for publishing that sort of content yourself. For example, clicking on 'Photos' will mean that you'll see all the photos and videos recently posted by your friends, but not links or music

RESOURCES

▶ Jargon Buster

Back-ups Copies of your family files; consider keeping a copy away from your home.

Blog An abbreviation of 'web log', a blog is an online journal used for all sorts of subjects.

BMD Births, Marriages and Deaths – the cornerstone of genealogical research.

Denization A denizen is a person who is permanently resident in another country but enjoys only certain rights of citizenship.

Drop-line chart Traditional style of family tree, showing earliest generations at the top and linking descendants vertically and horizontally.

Duplicates People recorded more than once in your family tree. This can happen after merging data from another file. Beware of just deleting one of the entries as this can disconnect one or more people.

File root Person chosen to be the focus of current family history research

GEDCOM Genealogical Data Communication – a standard file format that enables you to share information more easily between different family history programs.

General Register Office (GRO) The Government department responsible for the registration of births, marriages and deaths from 1837, and for the censuses from 1841.

Gregorian calendar Current system of recording dates, adopted in 1752.

International Genealogical Index (IGI) A large, comprehensive database of births and marriages gleaned from parish registers.

Julian calendar Date system used until 1752; be careful when studying records during the changeover from one calendar system to another.

Letters of Administration An official document that could be issued to surviving members of a family if their relative died intestate. In such a case, family members could apply for a Letter of Administration, entitling them to manage the estate.

Merge files Import information into your family tree, usually using GEDCOM.

Multimedia Refers to photographs, sound recordings and video clips that can be uploaded to your online family tree.

The National Archives The UK's principal repository for the United Kingdom based at Kew in Surrey. It contains over 11 million documents from the 11th century to the present. Records can be viewed at Kew, either in their original form or on microfiche/film, plus many are available online.

Naturalisation A naturalised person is permanently resident in another country and has been given citizenship.

PDF Portable Document File, used by professional publishers.

Pedigree chart Basic family tree showing vertical descendancy only.

Preferences The options in a family history program to set how the software operates. They typically contain choices for the date format and whether surnames are capitalised. You'll also find details of where to store back-ups within Preferences.

Primary source Original document, such as a birth, marriage or death certificate.

Relationships We all know about close relationships, but what is a second cousin twice removed? Most family history programs have a relationship calculator to work it out for you.

Repository Any library, archive or record office that holds family history records.

Secondary source Any records that have been compiled from primary sources. Secondary sources should always be checked against primary sources where possible, in case of errors and omissions.

▶ Common Abbreviations

COMMON ABBREVIATIONS

Here are some of the abbreviations you are most likely to come across in the course of your family history research.

Ag Lab	Agricultural Labourer
b.	Born
bach.	Bachelor
BL	British Library
bp. or bpt.	Baptised
BT	Bishop's Transcript
bur.	Buried
BVRI	The British Isles Vital Records Index
c.	Circa, or about
CARN	County Archives Record Network
coh.	Coheir(ess)
CRO	County record office
d.	Died
Diss.	Marriage dissolved/divorce
dsp	Died without issue
dvp	Died before father
d.yng.	Died young
ed.	Educated
fl.	Lived
FFHS	Federation of Family History Societies
FHS	Family History Society
GRO	General Register Office
IGI	The International Genealogical Index
inft	Infant
IWM	Imperial War Museum
kia	Killed in action
LDS	Church of Jesus Christ of Latter-Day Saints (Mormons)
M	Married
mar.	Marriage
MI	Monumental Inscriptions
miw	Mentioned in will of...
NAI	National Archives of Ireland
NRS	National Records of Scotland (formed by merger of NRS National Archives of Scotland and GROS General Register Office of Scotland)
Ob./Obit.	Died (less common than d.)
= or m.	Married
PCC	Prerogative Court of Canterbury
PRO	Public Record Office
PRONI	Public Record Office of Northern Ireland
SOG	Society of Genealogists

spin.	Spinster
TNA	The National Archives
unm.	Unmarried
w.pr.	Will proved

LATIN TERMS

Early documents may be written in Latin. Here are a few basic Latin terms to help you decipher them:

Annus	Year
Dies	Day
Est	Is
Filia	Daughter
Filius	Son
Mater	Mother
Matrimonium	Married
Mortuus	Died
Natus	Born
Nuptium	Married
Obit	Died
Pater	Father
Sepultat	Buried

Books

BOOKS

Essential reference guides
Dictionary of National Biography
The Phillimore Atlas and Index of Parish Registers
Burke's or *Debrett's Peerage*
Crockford's Clerical Directory

Internet research
Peter Christian *The Genealogists Internet* (The National Archives 2009)
Stuart A. Raymond *Netting Your Ancestors: Tracing Family History on the Internet* (The Family History Partnership 2007)

Other useful guides
Jonathan Brown *Tracing Your Rural Ancestors* (Pen and Sword Books 2011)
Mark Crail *Tracing Your Labour Movement Ancestors* (Pen and Sword Books 2009)
Simon Fowler *Tracing Your First World War Ancestors* (Countryside Books 2008)
Simon Fowler *Tracing Your Second World War Ancestors* (Countryside Books 2006)
Simon Fowler *Using Poor Law Records* (PRO Books 2001)
Karen Grunnan and Nigel Taylor *Wills and Probate Records*
David T. Hawkings *Criminal Ancestors* (The History Press 2009)
David T. Hawkings *Pauper Ancestors* (The History Press 2011)
David Hey *The Oxford Companion to Local and Family History* (OUP 2001)
David Hilliam *Kings, Queens, Bones and Bastards* (The History Press 2004)
Jennifer Newby *Women's Lives: Researching Women's Social History 1800–1939* (Pen and Sword Books 2011)
Stuart A. Raymond *Parish Registers, A History and Guide* (The Family History Partnership 2009)
Denis Stuart *Latin for Local and Family Historians* (Phillimore & Co 2006)
Colin Waters *Family History on the Net 2011/12* (Countryside Books 2011)
Rosemary Wenzerul *Tracing Your Jewish Ancestors* (Pen and Sword Books 2008)

Military

David Fletcher & Janice Tait *Tracing Your Tank Ancestors* (Pen and Sword Books 2011)

Simon Fowler *Tracing Your Army Ancestors* (Pen and Sword Books 2006)

Simon Fowler *Tracing Your Naval Ancestors* (Pen and Sword Books, 2011)

William Spencer *Air Force Records for Family Historians* (PRO Publications 2000)

William Spencer *Army Records: A Guide for Family Historians* (The National Archives 2008)

Phil Tomaselli *Tracing Your Air Force Ancestors* (Pen and Sword Books 2007)

Phil Tomaselli *Tracing Your Secret Service Ancestors* (Pen and Sword Books 2009)

Occupations

David T. Hawkings *Railway Ancestors* (The History Press 2008)

Michelle Higgs *Tracing Your Medical Ancestors* (Pen and Sword Books 2011)

Vivien Teasdale *Tracing Your Textile Ancestors* (Pen and Sword Books 2009)

English regions

Rachel Bellerby *Tracing Your Yorkshire Ancestors* (Pen and Sword Books 2006)

Jane Cox *Tracing Your East End Ancestors* (Pen and Sword Books 2011)

Dr Jonathan Oates *Tracing Your London Ancestors* (Pen and Sword Books 2011)

Mike Royden *Tracing Your Liverpool Ancestors* (Pen and Sword Books 2010)

Scotland

Bruce Drurie *Scottish Genealogy* (The History Press 2010)

Simon Fowler *Tracing Scottish Ancestors* (PRO Publications 2001)

Ian Maxwell *Tracing Your Scottish Ancestors* (Pen and Sword Books 2009)

Ireland

Simon Fowler *Tracing Irish Ancestors* (PRO Publications 2002)

Ian Maxwell *Your Irish Ancestors: A Guide for Family Historians* (Pen and Sword Books 2008)

CDs

Many of the standard indexes, as well as county guides, are available on CD from suppliers such as S&N Genealogy (see page 218)

▶ Useful Websites

USEFUL WEBSITES

Starting out

Archives Hub
Details of archives held by
universities and colleges in the UK
www.archiveshub.ac.uk

British Genealogy
Comprehensive guide to family
history resources
www.british-genealogy.com

Cindy's List
Brilliant community site, with links
to a wide range of topics
www.cindyslist.com

FamilySearch.org
The official website of the Church
of Jesus Christ of Latter-Day
Saints – contains a wealth of useful
information
www.familysearch.org

The Genealogist
Various useful online databases
and transcripts, including censuses
www.thegenealogist.co.uk

General Register Office
Official government site for
ordering birth, marriage and death
certificates
www.gro.gov.uk/gro/content/
certificates/default.asp

Genuki
Links to counties of the UK, as well
as specific topics
www.genuki.org.uk

The National Archives
One of the largest repositories
in the UK, and the essential
starting point for any family history
research
www.nationalarchives.gov.uk

Society of Genealogists
Has an extensive library covering
all aspects of genealogy; catalogue
is searchable online.
www.sog.org.uk

Libraries

British Library Family History
Help with finding essential
resources for family history
www.bl.uk/familyhistory.html

British Library Newspapers
Searchable catalogue of vast
collection of British newspapers,
magazines, journals and comics
http://newspapers.bl.uk

The Wellcome Library
Searchable online catalogue of
historical medical records
http://library.wellcome.ac.uk

Northern Ireland

Census of Ireland, 1901 and 1911
Ongoing project to put the census
records of 1901 and 1911 online;
now almost completed. Covers
all 32 counties of Ireland: www.
census.nationalarchives.ie

National Archives of Ireland
http://nationalarchives.ie/

**Public Record Office of Northern
Ireland**
Northern Ireland's major archive.
Includes names of landholders and
Ulster covenant signatories
www.proni.gov.uk

Scotland

Ancestral Scotland
Useful family history links, with a section on Scottish clans; a good starting point for those researching Scottish roots
www.ancestralscotland.com

National Records of Scotland
Formed in April 2011 from the merger of the National Archives of Scotland and the General Register Office for Scotland. A new website is in the pipeline; until its launch, you can still use www.nas.gov.uk

Scotlands People
The official government site for Scottish family history; search statutory records, old parish registers, census records, Catholic records, wills and testaments and coats of arms
www.scotlandspeople.gov.uk

Wales

Archives Wales
Details of archives in Wales, with a searchable catalogue
www.archiveswales.org.uk

National Library of Wales
The main family history resource for Wales
www.llgc.org.uk

Subscription sites

Ancestry
www.ancestry.co.uk

Find My Past
www.findmypast.co.uk

Origins
Extensive collection of British and Irish records from the 13th century to the present
www.origins.net

Birth, marriage and death

Commonwealth War Graves Commission
www.cwgc.org

Free BMD
www.freebmd.org.uk

The Gravestone Project
Ongoing project to photograph and transcribe Monumental Inscriptions from around the world. Free searches
www.gravestonephotos.com

Census records

FreeCen
www.freecen.org.uk

1901 Census Online
www.1901censusonline.com

1911 Census Online
www.1911census.co.uk

Adoption

Barnardo's Family Connections
Records of children adopted through Barnardo's homes.
www.barnardos.org.uk/familyconnections.htm

British Home Children
A site dedicated to the child emigration scheme to Canada, 1870–1957
http://freepages.genealogy.rootsweb.ancestry.com/~britishhomechildren/

▷ Useful Websites

Immigration and emigration
Ancestors on Board
Passenger lists of people leaving
Britain between 1890 and 1960
www.ancestorsonboard.com

Moving Here
Site dedicated to immigrants,
which includes help with tracing
family roots
www.movinghere.org.uk

Military history
Army Museums Ogilby Trust
www.armymuseums.org.uk

Imperial War Museum
www.iwm.org.uk

National Army Museum
www.national-army-museum.ac.uk

RAF Museum
www.rafmuseum.org.uk

Online family tree builders
Family Relatives
www.familyrelatives.com

GenesReunited
Classic family tree linking website
with 500 million names.
www.genesreunited.com

Online forums
British Genealogy
www.british-genealogy.com

Roots Web
www.rootsweb.com

Other useful sites
Black Sheep Ancestors
www.blacksheepancestors.com/uk

Burke's Peerage
For tracing royal or aristocratic
ancestors
www.burkespeerage.com

Cornucopia
Online searchable database of
more than 6000 collections in UK
museums, galleries and archives
www.cornucopia.org.uk

**Federation of Family History
Societies**
Details of family history societies
throughout the UK, with
information on how to join, services
offered, publications, meetings and
events, and links to useful sites
www.ffhs.org.uk

Lost Ancestors
www.ffhs.org.uk/projects/strays.
php

Missing Ancestors
www.missing-ancestors.com

UK Birth Adoption Register
www.ukbirth-adoptionregister.com

Overseas archives
Archives Canada
www.archivescanada.ca

**Directory of Archives New
Zealand**
http://archives.govt.nz/

**India Office Family History
Search**
http://indiafamily.bl.uk/UI

National Archives of Australia
www.naa.gov.au

**The US National Archives and
Records Administration**
www.archives.gov/research

Genealogical supplies
S&N Genealogy
www.genealogysupplies.com

Index

ABOUT THE CONSULTANT EDITOR NICOLA LISLE
Nicola Lisle is a freelance journalist who specialises in family history and the arts, and has written extensively for *Family History Monthly* and *Ancestors*.

FAMILY HISTORIAN STARTER EDITION 4.1

The CD-Rom included with this book features a starter pack of family tree software, Family Historian Starter Edition 4.1, so you can start building your family tree on your PC. Using Family Historian Starter Edition 4.1, you can add up to 80 people per GEDCOM file (see pages 176–9), add photos (see pages 180–1), video and audio to your family tree, and share it with others (see pages 182–7), as well as much more.

To install Family Historian Starter Edition 4.1 from the CD-Rom, you will need a PC with the minimum system requirements listed below:

1 Insert the CD-Rom into your PC's disc drive.
2 A welcome page will open up in your web browser. Read the terms and conditions, and if you are happy with them, click **Install Family Historian Starter Edition 4.1** and follow the instructions on-screen.
3 Once the software is installed, a shortcut icon will appear on your desktop. Double click this to open the software.

If the CD-Rom doesn't run automatically when inserted into your PC's disc drive, select the **Run** command from the 'Start' menu (under Accessories in some versions of Windows). Most disc drives are drive D, so type D:\Start and click **OK**. (If your disc drive is not drive D, substitute the correct drive letter.)

More advice on starting to build your family tree is available once you have installed the software. Click **Tips for New & Upgrading Users** on the first screen that appears. Advice and instructions for using Family Historian Starter Edition 4.1 can also be found by clicking **Help** on the menu bar within the software.

To upgrade to the full version of Family Historian, click **Buy the Full Version of Family Historian** within the 'Help' menu of the software.

> ## System requirements
> Operating system – Microsoft Windows 7, Vista, or XP
> Memory – at least 40 MB of available hard drive space